Christian life today. Merton himself would chuckle about it, but he would take delight in the fact that a young Baptist minister would understand so well and cherish his concern for contemplation in a world of action.

—E. GLENN HINSON
Retired senior professor of Church History and Spirituality;
friend of Thomas Merton;
and author of *Miracle of Grace*

I0151491

HS
SMYTH&
HELWYS

Smyth & Helwys Publishing, Inc.
6316 Peake Road
Macon, Georgia 31210-3960
1-800-747-3016
©2014 by Bert Montgomery

Cover illustration by Greg Cravens

Library of Congress Cataloging-in-Publication Data

Montgomery, Bert.
Of mice and ministers / by Bert Montgomery.
pages cm
Includes bibliographical references.
ISBN 978-1-57312-733-2 (pbk. : alk. paper)
1. Popular culture--Religious aspects--Christianity.
2. Popular music--Religious aspects--Christianity. I. Title.
BR115.C8M6473 2014
261--dc23

2014018618

Praise for *Of Mice and Ministers*

With wry humor and ridiculous puns, Bert Montgomery's writing delivers a chuckle, but you may also find yourself surprised by the sharp edges of the gospel poking through his stories and deflating your pipe dreams of what it means to be a follower of Jesus. In his reflections, Bert gathers up popular (and unpopular) music, stories and interviews punctuated with irony, and Scriptures accented by a Southern drawl. He spins every tale in the light of God's mercy and grace and leaves his readers with lots to ponder.

—EILEEN CAMPBELL-REED
Practical Theologian and Co-director of the
Learning Pastoral Imagination Project

I have been fortunate to share a planet with great writers, speakers, and teachers—from Tony Campolo and Ron Sider to the late Mike Yaconelli. Bert Montgomery has the same skills and gifts of bringing alive a message of life, love, faith, and culture as the above mentioned men. With humor and insight, Bert connects the person in the pulpit to the person in the pew, auditorium, or classroom, and does so in a way that sends one out the door thinking, "I can make God's creation a better place with my life."

—BRIAN HEALY
Lead singer, Dead Artist Syndrome

For Bert Montgomery, revelation is not confined to domesticated readings of popular Bible verses. In *Of Mice and Ministers*, he invites complicated biblical characters and earthy people into conversation with contemporary issues and cultural icons. With both humor and poignancy, Bert shares his pastoral imagination and his keen eye for seeing the holy all around us.

—DALEN C. JACKSON
Academic Dean and Professor of Biblical Studies
Baptist Seminary of Kentucky

No one listens better for the voice of God in the noise and clatter of life than Bert Montgomery. He listens to musicians, artists, poor folk, rich folk, a few overtly religious folk, his own heart, and even Jesus. Then, somehow, he distills what he thinks he has heard into some of the finest essays and interviews imaginable. When you read *Of Mice and Ministers*, you'll be moved to laugh, cry, get angry, enter into despair, and yet hope that Jesus is still alive and at work in all the arenas of life.

Bert is an honest writer. That is, he writes what he feels to be true, raises questions he believes need to be raised, leaves hanging matters he cannot resolve, and states conclusions that are his own. He is not for sale. Even if you find yourself disagreeing with him at times, you'll come away from *Of Mice and Ministers* enriched by engagement with his lively mind and generous heart.

Of Mice and Ministers is on my personal list of the "Top Ten" books I've read this year. The only books that make that list are those I find worth reading not once but several times, with each reading revealing yet another layer of insight and meaning.

—MICHAEL A. SMITH
Senior pastor, Central Baptist Church of Fountain City and
Co-author of *Mount and Mountain*

[Bert's] wit and insights are as refreshing as hand-churned ice cream—a delight to savor.

—KAREN SPEARS ZACHARIAS
Author of *Mother of Rain*, *Will Jesus Buy Me a Double-Wide?*,
and *After the Flag Has Been Folded*

Praise for "A Baptist Preacher Sits Down with Everyone's Favorite Deceased Monk"

Bert Montgomery has opened a fresh, wise, conversational way for Thomas Merton to speak anew to our time. Somebody should put this on stage and invite the audience to join in.

—LOYD ALLEN
Professor of Formation
McAfee School of Theology (Mercer University)

Bert's post-mort interview with T-Mert is one for the ages.

—ROBERT DARDEN
Formerly senior editor of *The* [late, great] *Wittenburg Door*

What a wonderful way to get before others some of Thomas Merton's keen insights into the malaise of our society and ways to rethink the

Of Mice and Ministers

Musings and Conversations about Life, Death,
Grace, and Everything

Bert Montgomery

To Jency,

always supporting,
always encouraging,
always hoping,
always praying,
and always loving . . .

Author's Note

As with my previous collections of musings, most everything found in this book was featured previously at various online sites. Two (almost three) of the interviews in Part II were actually published elsewhere and appear, with permission, in this assemblage. I am thankful for the following websites for giving space to my musings and interviews:

www.thefaithlab.info
www.burnsidewriters.com
www.redletterchristians.org
www.huffingtonpost.com

Also, Daniel Bailey has graciously consented to share his song "Burden of Belief"—which inspired my musing, aptly titled "Burden of Belief"—with readers of this book and with anyone who visits my website. Simply go to www.bertmontgomery.com and look for the Daniel Bailey "Burden of Belief" free mp3 download! (Thanks, Mr. Bailey!)

Finally, thanks to my friends at TheFaithLab for my website, and to my friends at Smyth & Helwys for yet another book (if you keep publishing 'em, I'll keep writing 'em!).

—Bert
May 2014

Also by Bert Montgomery

Bert Montgomery
Elvis, Willie, Jesus & Me

The Musings and Mutterings of a Church Misfit

Bert Montgomery
Psychic Pancakes & Communion Pizza

More Musings and Mutterings of a Church Misfit

These and other titles available from www.helwys.com

Contents

Foreword

When a Baptist pastor named Bert Montgomery, whom I met on Facebook, invited me—a dropout from both Contemporary Christian Music and organized church—to drive from Nashville to Starkville, Mississippi, and share my painful story about spiritual, mental, and physical abuse at the hands of a misogynistic hierarchical version of the "Christian" church, I incredulously asked, "Are you *crazy?*" He replied, "Yes . . . but *pretty please?* My congregation needs to hear your story." So one Sunday morning, instead of Bert preaching, I shared my songs and my story, including my song "Angry Woman."

Bert's approach to culture, spirituality, theology, God, and community reminds me of that incredibly eccentric Southern artist, Howard Finster, who took all things broken—bottles, dishes, tools, furniture, paintings, anything discarded—and turned it all into art and installed it in its own place of honor in his yard. People traveled hundreds of miles to experience his outside gallery. It was Finster's great visual proclamation of the gospel: of how God takes everything broken and makes it into something interesting, if not beautiful!

That's exactly what Bert does with his writing. It's whimsical; it's serious; it's inclusive; it welcomes questions and ideas. No one—not right-wing Republicans, leftist Democrats, atheists, gays, lesbians, transgenders, heterosexuals, Muslims, Christians, Hindus, country or rap artists, or even angry women—threatens his relationship with God because his God is bigger than all of our notions.

Bert Montgomery changed the direction of my life because he celebrated the symbolic "Angry Woman" inside all of us, knowing that the only way out is through it: to experience, embrace, and offer forgiveness. He's thought provoking and a whole lot of fun to read; you never know where he's going to take you next. The stories may appear to have nothing to do with one another, but ultimately, they are all gathered up into that seamless net of God's grace.

I knew Bert was eccentric when part of my payment was dinner at the best pizza place in town, and when he asked his son to sleep on the sofa so I could have a bedroom. Jesus said that the "truth will set you free," and I think Bert has made it out of the birdcage.

—*Pam Mark Hall*
www.pammarkhall.com
April 2014

Part 1

Musings & Such

Of "Lights" and Soul Liberation

(Confessions from a Real-life Journey Moment)

"Honey, thou dost protest too much, methinks."

My wife says this frequently. Oh, she's not always so Shakespearean about it, but she does essentially say that.

Denial is a funny thing. Refusing to accept the truth about yourself often leads to projecting your loathing upon others. Plus, it's hard to love others if you don't love yourself, and it's tough to love yourself when you hate things about yourself.

I recently sat down with my friend Jimmy Arnold, a professional musician who can play the guitar and sing like nobody's business. And he's a just an all-around great guy. There we were in a Memphis restaurant talking music and spirituality, and he started telling me about his own spiritual journey, which included a few stories about his longtime friend Jonathan Cain.

Yes, *that* Jonathan Cain—the Journey keyboardist who co-wrote such hits as "Faithfully," "Open Arms" (my wife's prom song), and everyone's favorite anthem, "Don't Stop Believin'."

For the record,[1] I despise Journey. I've been despising them for over thirty years of my life. Ask my wife; she's put up with my obnoxious rants against anything related to Journey for twenty-five of those years. Ask anyone who's ever tried to listen to or, heaven forbid, sing along with a Journey song in my presence.

Yet here I sat with my friend, Jimmy, who is friends with a leader in this band I love to hate. Jimmy played guitar in the late 1970s in Jonathan Cain's band.[2] It took me a couple of weeks to bring it up, but soon I began an Internet conversation with Jimmy about Journey—

online therapy, if you will. I began working out a deep dark secret of mine ("Liberating my soul," Jimmy called it).

My "liberation" began by confessing to Jimmy that I've secretly been enjoying Journey since my junior high years (1980–1982). Outwardly, though, I loved hating them. My confession will come as no surprise to my wife and sons, who've asked me many times that if I hate Journey so much, why do I insist on singing along with them on the radio? And just why, exactly, do I know all the words?

"I think any music/art that shines a light on darkness is totally valid regardless of style or popularity," Jimmy reassuringly responded. "Touching others in a way that brings light to their lives is the noblest of goals. Of course, the same logic holds true for all areas of our lives. Our job is to reflect the light within us . . . ."

Jimmy grew up Catholic, but he sure sounded like some of my favorite Quaker writers with his response.

You know, in a way, it really is a form of soul liberation. Jesus says that I am to love my neighbor as I love myself; and hating myself for secretly liking Journey has surely projected itself negatively in my relationships with others.

Thanks to Jimmy, with whom I had a real-life "Journey moment," I am learning to love myself by accepting the fact that I enjoy Journey. Maybe I'll become a little less judgmental and a little more loving toward others as a result.

Now, if you'll excuse me, all of this Quaker-like talk of "Light" has made me want to sing, well, a Journey song. Feel free to join me and sing along: "When the lights go down in the city . . . ."[3]

Notes

1. "For the record" . . . record, get it? Journey? Music? Yes, the pun was very much intended.

2. The name of Jonathan Cain's band featuring Jimmy Arnold was—wait for it—the Jonathan Cain Band.

3. That's pronounced "sit-taaayyyy."

If You Wanna Get to Heaven, You Might Wanna Listen to the Ozark Mountain Daredevils

(Ode to Dale and Mary)

Dale and I became fast friends a few years ago because of our love for the music of the Missouri band of rural hippie farmers known as the Ozark Mountain Daredevils. Their song "Beauty in the River" is one of my all-time favorite hymns.[1]

> *there's a beauty in the river*
> *there's a beauty in the stream*
> *there's a beauty in the forest at night*
> *when the lonely nightbird screams*

Dale and his wife, Mary, loved the song "Beauty in the River" so much that the lyrics were printed on the back of their 1979 wedding program. He and his groomsmen even sang it after the ceremony.

> *there's a truth in the eyes of my woman*
> *that no mortal ever knew*
> *she lights my way like the coming of the day*
> *when the sun shines on the dew*

Dale told me he always joked with Mary that since he sang to her at their wedding, he'd also sing at her funeral if he got the chance.

and there's so much time for livin'
and so much time to die
there's so much time for laughin'
and so much time to cry

Dale lost Mary and one of their daughters in a car wreck the day after Christmas in 2005; the lyrics to "Beauty in the River" were printed in Mary's funeral bulletin. Dale did his best to sing it at her visitation.

"It was probably one of the hardest, most emotional, and coolest things I ever did."

we must all stand in the water
we must find it when we roam
it don't matter what is said
we can wake up from the dead
and roll away the stone

Words from the Ozark Mountain Daredevils are forever treasured in Dale's heart. They don't explain the death of his wife and daughter, and I doubt they ease the pain much, but for Dale they are far, far more than song lyrics. They reach down, down, down into the mystery of his soul where words and understanding cease to exist; where his spirit speaks mysteriously with the Spirit of God; where somehow, someway Dale senses that his wife and daughter aren't really lost to him after all.

From the same band that gives us the foot-stompin' anthem "If You Wanna Get to Heaven"[2] and the always exciting "Chicken Train,"[3] we also get the worshipful "Beauty in the River."

we must all stand in the water
we must find it when we roam
it don't matter what is said
we can wake up from the dead
and roll away the stone

I love the Ozark Mountain Daredevils, and I'm thankful that God doesn't rely solely on respectable, proper, seminary-trained professional clergy to speak to us.[4]

For Dale, there's a connection with the Daredevils that goes beyond a catchy tune and great lyrics. It's a connection that is at once bookends marking the physical beginning and the end of a stage of his journey. At the same time it is a connection with the Eternal that transcends time, space, understanding, and even life and death.

You can say what you want about God and the Ozark Mountain Daredevils, but I trust Dale. Besides, as Dale himself will tell you,

it don't matter what is said
we can wake up from the dead
and roll away the stone . . .
Hallelujah!

Notes

1. Of the "not-actually-a-hymn" variety, that is. "Beauty in the River" was written by John Dillon and recorded by the Ozark Mountain Daredevils on their magnificent 1973 eponymous debut album from A&M Records.

2. According to the Daredevils, "if you wanna get to heaven, you gotta raise a little hell."

3. Sing along if you know the words: "laser beam . . . in my dream . . . ."

4. As a seminary-trained, sort-of-professional clergyperson myself, I confess that the Daredevils are just a whole lot more fun.

How to Satisfy Jesus

(via the Gospel of Elvis)

I wish I had a nickel for every time God spoke to me through Elvis, like in the Elvis song "A Little Less Conversation":[1]

A little less conversation, a little more action please;
All this aggravation ain't satisfactionin' me;
A little more bite and a little less bark;
A little less fight and a little more spark;
Close your mouth and open up your heart, and satisfy me.

Sure, on the surface it's just another Elvis song pleading with a woman for some more active lovin', but when paired with the Gospels, with repeated teachings of Jesus, and particularly Jesus' parable of the sheep and the goats,[2] it's just as clearly a song that can be heard as Jesus' pleading with the church for some more active, well, lovin'.

Mohandas Gandhi read the Gospels, particularly the Sermon on the Mount, and was forever changed. Jesus was the Way to follow! But you know the rest of the story: Gandhi looked up and saw the British Empire with swords drawn, oppressing and exploiting the people and the land of his beloved India, all in the name of Christianity.

Gandhi declared that he, therefore, could not be a Christian.

Novelist Anne Rice not long ago became a Christian; she turned her attention to writing fiction about Jesus' childhood. Everybody was so excited that the novelist known for her incredibly dark vampire stories had become a Christian . . . until not-so-not-so long ago, when she publicly stated that she quit being a Christian because she'd rather follow Christ.

One cannot help wondering if Jesus, like Gandhi and Anne Rice, would look around at popular Christianity today and say, "If *this* is Christianity, then . . . ."

What would happen if—referring to Americanized Christianity—we all asked, "What would Jesus do?"

Imagine Jesus sitting in the wings at one of our big, stadium-filled "I'm-a-Christian" prayer celebrations, when a superstar walks up to the microphone and reads from Matthew's Gospel, chapter 25:

> Then the king will say to those on his right hand, "Come, you that are blessed by my Father, inherit this great kingdom prepared for you by your founding fathers, for I was a Christian politician, and you voted for me; for I was a Christian businessman, and you spent your money at my store to support 'Kingdom Values'; I was a cute slogan bumper sticker, and you proudly put me on your car; I was a bill protecting 'Christian values,' and you helped to get me enacted into law . . . .'"

Of course, that's not what Matthew 25 actually says. It's about feeding the hungry, welcoming the stranger, caring for the sick, visiting the prisoner—about how any time we do anything for "the least of these," we are serving Jesus himself; and when we don't do anything for "the least of these," we're actually turning away from Jesus himself.

Many are familiar with the song that goes, "They will know we are Christians by our love." We've been taught in our churches, though, that what that really means is "They will know we are Christians by our loud boasting."

A Christian athlete recently shared his testimony with a group of local students. The athlete spoke of hard decisions he has had to make as a Christian. He spoke sincerely of tough choices that tested his commitment to his Christian faith.

The athlete talked about his friend who, after a lot of struggling, decided that she was gay. The athlete wondered what he should do; he remembered the story of Jonah—how when Jonah was running from God and was on the ship, the crew of the ship threw Jonah overboard. Thus, the athlete shared that it was his Christian duty to "throw" his friend "overboard," meaning he couldn't be her friend anymore based on her sexuality.

The Christian culture we live in teaches us how to talk a lot about Jesus, but it has hardly anything to do with helping us learn how to love like Jesus. Would Jesus throw someone overboard? Of course not! Our churches, though, teach us how to throw all kinds of people overboard every day.[3]

It doesn't take long to conclude that if Jesus stood here today, he might well say, "If this is Christianity, then I am *not* a Christian."

When it comes to a Christ-like message, much in keeping with the sheep and the goats, few things can match the simple message of Elvis's hit, "A Little Less Conversation."

Want to serve Jesus? Talk less; love more. Want to follow Christ? Close your mouth and open up your heart.

"Satisfy me, Baby!"[4]

Notes

1. Elvis recorded the song, written by Mac Davis and Billy Strange, in 1968.

2. Matthew 25:31-46. Warning: This story isn't for the faint of heart or for those who long for a comfortable faith focusing only on the afterlife.

3. Not to mention that this was also a terrible misuse of the Jonah story, which actually teaches that God is not limited or confined by our own prejudices and beliefs, no matter how convinced we are that we're standing firm on God's very words.

4. The word of the Lord (paraphrased via Elvis). Thanks be to God!

We're Gonna Need a Bigger Boat!

(Ode to *Jaws* and Fishing for Men)

Quint the fisherman, played to perfection by the scene-stealing Robert Shaw in the 1975 Steven Spielberg masterpiece, *Jaws*, was a rugged, thick-skinned, and independent man who played by his own rules and offered to hunt, kill, and bring back to shore the shark that was terrorizing a small coastal town—for the right price, of course.

I've met some fishermen like Mr. Quint down on Louisiana's Gulf Coast. You'd have to be tough and unlikable to some degree to choose to live alone or in small groups out on the open waters, far from shore, with little or no shelter from the terrible storms.

"Come, follow me!" says Jesus to some Quint-like fishermen along the Sea of Galilee.

"Come, follow me, and I will make you fishers of men!"

Mark's Gospel simply records that two sets of brothers dropped what they were doing and walked away from their boats to follow Jesus.

Perhaps Mark writes so matter-of-factly because he dares not record the salty language of the future disciples, nor the extra-salty language of their families and co-fishermen as they watched promising young men throwing their lives, as well as their nets, away.

"Come, follow me, and I will make you fishers of men!"

And there we have it. Some two thousand years later, a powerful image of the mission of God has become little more than a slick marketing scheme.

It was inevitable, really. The slow, generation-after-generation-after-generation evolutionary growth of individualism, coinciding with the growth of crass commercialism, consumerism, and salesmanship, has altered not only our world economies and our habits of buying and selling but also our very relationships with each other and with God.

Quite naturally, then, the general "popular" understanding of this Scripture has been, in light of our American marketing DNA, individualistic and consumeristic.[1]

"Fishing for men" has come to mean delivering a hard sales pitch and pressing to meet a salvation/baptism quota. So many of our churches and denominations and campus ministries and such have made the good news of the kingdom of God into not much more than a wiggling worm impaled on a fishing hook.

Like the fancy money-back-guaranteed lures in the sport of recreational fishing, the sport of Christian evangelism has evolved from the simple-yet-effective sales pitch—"If you got hit by a bus when you walked out of here this morning, do you know where you would go when you died?"—into the high-tech lures of smoke and fog machines, rock music, free pizza parties,[2] and hell houses.[3]

You can insert your own joke and/or personal story of how difficult it is to tell the difference between a preacher and a used-car salesman here; everybody has one.

The whole idea of fishing with lures as an example of Christian witness is appalling. Maybe it's because I still have the hook scars in my cheeks from having bitten the bait many a time in my youth, not to mention going through more than one form of the "proper training" to be an effective salesman.[4]

Jesus doesn't mention lures and bait, or people—like fish—being tricked into biting a line and swallowing hook, line, and sinker.

Being "fishers of men" is not about getting people to take our bait. It's about casting huge nets of grace and bringing all the people within our reach along with us into the current of God's kingdom as it manifests itself on earth as it is in heaven.

Like Mr. Quint in *Jaws*, and the folks who fish on their boats off Grand Isle, Louisiana, this kind of fishing Jesus talked about isn't very clean or very easy or easily measurable by bookkeeping standards.

Casting wide nets and bringing people along in the grace of God is not for the faint of heart. It can be dangerous, and many of Jesus' grace fishermen have met the same fate of Mr. Quint in *Jaws*. Think

Dietrich Bonhoeffer. Think Martin Luther King, Jr. Oh, and think Jesus himself.

But one thing is for sure: these little vessels (er, church buildings) we've constructed—no matter how big or how small or how mega-sized—tend to be designed for sporting evangelism.

If we're going to follow Jesus and cast his deep and wide net of God's grace, we're "gonna need a bigger boat." God's kingdom is a boat more than big enough to carry you, and me, and them, and those other folks, and even those folks over there, and the ones we love, and the ones we don't love . . . .

Please excuse me; it's time for my devotional. Now, where's my *Jaws* DVD?

Notes

1. Consumeristic? . . . Consumerist? . . . Consumer-oriented? . . . Whatever. Back to the story.

2. "Free" as used here means having to sit and listen to a guilt-hurling evangelist.

3. "Hell houses" being the so-called "Christian" alternative to Halloween haunted houses—both of which aim to scare the hell out of you.

4. Oops—I mean "evangelist."

Never Mind the Nonsense

(Ode to Jesus & Johnny Rotten)

At the end of his final live show with his band the Sex Pistols, the notorious, belligerent, somewhat anti-social punk rocker Johnny Rotten yelled out to the audience, "Ever get the feeling you've been cheated?" Rotten walked off the stage and left the band, and the Sex Pistols soon completely disintegrated.

So, ever get the feeling you've been cheated?

We want life to be fair. We want to know, we want a guarantee, that if we keep our end of the bargain, the other parties are going to keep their end of the bargain.

If we feel that we have been cheated, there are all sorts of clearly defined procedures we can follow to register a complaint and have it examined by an official.

A student who believes she has been graded unfairly and in a manner not in keeping with the syllabus grading scheme can register a complaint with the school and have someone look into the matter. A customer who believes he received a less-than-satisfactory product can ask to speak to a manager, or send a complaint to someone in a corporate office, and have the issue analyzed. American citizens who feel that a particular law or court ruling is unfair to them can join together and have lawyers argue their case all the way up to the Supreme Court.

Why do we do these things? Because in all areas of life there are times when, whether or not we actually have, we get the feeling that we've been cheated.

Jesus tells a parable about workers in a vineyard. These workers worked all day and expected a full-day's wage . . . and they received it (see Matt 20:1-16).

But there were also workers who got hired later and only worked half the day, and, worse, workers who got hired at the end of the day and only worked one hour. Even so, at the end of the day when the money started being distributed, the last ones hired got paid first, and they got a full day's pay, then the half-day workers got a full day's pay, and, finally, the all-day workers—you guessed it—got a full-day's pay.

The all-day workers, naturally, complained because they felt cheated. This is what the kingdom of God is like, Jesus says: grace doesn't always appear fair.

Have you felt resentment toward the grace that has been poured out on another person who is obviously less deserving, when you've been doing good all along? Ever get the feeling you've been cheated?

A single mother finds her way into a local church, and the church takes her and her child in warmly. She volunteers and helps often around the church and participates in functions. After a while, she is asked to help co-direct the church nursery.

A longtime member of the church, one of the most loyal and hardworking people there, complains to the pastor. That woman has no business helping in a leadership role with the children. She's unmarried. Her life has been a mess. She still doesn't have it all together. So what if she's good with the kids? What kind of example is it if the church starts letting just anybody come in and start leading?

The longtime member is feeling more than a bit cheated: cheated over leadership issues (why hasn't *she* been asked to be in a leadership role?) but also cheated because of grace. This single mother has a not-very-polite past and occasionally a still-not-very-polite present, and yet grace is being poured out on her as equally as to the longtime member.

In Jesus' kingdom in which a Johnny Rotten is as welcomed and loved as a Bill Gaither, instead of complaining about being cheated, give thanks; for somewhere, somebody is complaining that she's been cheated because you've been treated equally to her.

Never mind the religious nonsense. Here's to God's cheating grace!

Politics, Prejudices, and Hungry Dogs

It was a cold and drizzling Easter Sunday morning, early just before sunrise, in rural northern Kentucky. I was assisting the local Methodist pastor in leading the community sunrise Easter service.

Reverend Davenport decided to serve Communion to everyone in attendance at the conclusion of his devotional. He had with him a freshly baked loaf of bread, a chalice of grape juice, and a small fire around which we gathered to keep warm.

As Reverend Davenport read from the Scriptures, a mangy, stray dog started sniffing around all of us; the pastor never noticed as the dog came right up behind him and me, but I saw the dog grab that freshly baked loaf of bread in his jaws and run off with it. He didn't even leave any crumbs for us, the children of God. The whole loaf—the Body of Christ—was literally wasted on one nasty dog that day.

Jesus talks about wasting good stuff on dogs. In one place he says, "Do not give what is holy to dogs; and do not throw your pearls before swine, or they will trample them under foot and turn and maul you" (Matt 7:6). Later, a Canaanite woman asks Jesus for help, and Jesus replies, "I was sent only to the lost sheep of the house of Israel." He goes on to suggest that choosing to help the woman would be like throwing the children's food to the dogs (see Matt 15:21-28).

"Dogs" was an easily recognizable term in Jesus' day. It was often used to describe people considered undesirable, lesser than, unworthy.

Clarence Jordan, translator of the Gospels into the language and customs of the mid-1900s American South, has a black woman come to Jesus, and Jesus says, "I was sent only to needy white people"; hence, he shouldn't throw the children's food to the puppies.

Culture and politics sure can influence how we view one another, even as people of faith. Listen to our conversations about immigration; we are good at classifying groups of people and speaking of each other in terms of categories rather than as humans.

A plane wreck happened in 1948; the radio and newspaper coverage identified the flight crew and the security guard and then labeled the Mexican migrant farm workers who were being flown back to Mexico simply as "deportees." This incident became a powerful song by Woody Guthrie, who turned it into a symbol of the way categories can desensitize us to the humanness of others.

> Goodbye to my Juan, goodbye, Rosalita,
> Adios mis amigos, Jesus y Maria;
> You won't have your names when you ride the big airplane,
> All they will call you will be "deportees."[1]

Maybe we would do well to stop trying to analyze and dissect and explain to our satisfaction why Jesus would compare the woman in this story to dogs. Maybe it's best that we see the whole picture in its context. When Jesus spoke to her in what were completely acceptable terms for his culture, he was among his followers and disciples, who probably would have called her much worse. He acknowledged their prejudices and their sense of superiority in his words to her, and then he shocked them all by acting on behalf of, well, "the dog."

Most of us in the American church today will not use words to clump entire groups of people into a category as a way of dehumanizing them. Most of us today will not use words like "nigger," "white trash," "spic," "gook," "towelhead," "faggot," or "illegal immigrant" to help us cloud the human faces staring back at us. Or do you object that a particular term was included in this offensive list?

How soon we forget that, despite our well-publicized adoration of Jesus, in Matthew's story we are not the disciples or the other followers of Jesus; most of us are the Canaanite woman. *We American Christians are the cultural "dogs"!* In this context, when Jesus speaks of not giving what is holy to the dogs and wasting the children's food on the dogs, he's not teaching us to be careful with whom we share our grace and our resources; he's playing into the cultural prejudices of his followers and then is going to shock them by sharing grace and resources with us.

And, like that dog on a rainy Kentucky Easter morning, we now find that we have not the crumbs but the whole loaf of God's grace.

Pay attention each and every election season. Candidates will try to publicly "out-love" Jesus more than the next candidate, and many of us Christians will be more than eager to indulge in self-righteous displays on behalf of our favorite candidate. But listen to how we categorize people. Pay attention to how we see fewer human faces and more groupings of undesirable objects.

And remember that we have been the cultural dogs that received holy grace from Jesus. May we then extend the same grace and resources to those who are deemed "dogs" in our culture today, for Jesus freely gives to these "dogs" the whole loaf of Communion bread—his very Body—in spite of what our politics and our cultural prejudices demand.

Note

1. Woody Guthrie's copyright for the song "Plane Wreck at Los Gatos" was renewed in 1961.

Jesus in a '49 Ford

(Ode to Marshall Grant and the Statler Brothers)

Music legend Marshall Grant, an original member of Johnny Cash's backing band the Tennessee Three, died on August 7, 2011. I had the honor of meeting him about three years before that at the Johnny Cash Flower-Pickin' Festival in Starkville.

After a lengthy time of touring with Cash and acting as his road manager, Grant went on to manage the career of another Cash act, the Statler Brothers. Throughout the 1970s and into the 1980s, the Statler Brothers were one of the best-selling groups in country music.[1]

While Grant was managing them, they wrote and sang a song titled "Would You Recognize Jesus?"[2]

> *Would you recognize Jesus if you met him face to face;*
> *or would you wonder if He's just someone you couldn't place?*
> *You may not find Him coming in a chariot of the Lord*
> *Jesus could be riding in a '49 Ford.*

The 2005 Cooperative Baptist Fellowship General Assembly was just plain weird. Rather than being—like most conventions—centered downtown in a major city with hotels clustered around a convention center, this particular one was at a new self-contained convention center/resort complex outside of Dallas in Grapevine, Texas. The Gaylord Texan is the name of this luxurious world unto itself.

Here were thousands of Cooperative Baptists, largely white middle-class folks, going to conferences and attending sessions challenging us to address poverty issues and racial issues and justice issues from the pulpit, in Sunday school classes, and in our individual and collective actions. Visually, the contrast was overwhelming: white folks wanting to serve God, follow Christ, and deal with poverty and racism being served and spoiled and pampered by hundreds and hundreds and hundreds of Hispanic workers.

Hispanics—some speaking very little English—making our beds. Carrying our luggage. Waiting our tables. Cleaning our bathrooms. Picking up our trash. Bringing us our extravagantly overpriced "luxurious" foods and drinks.

I attended the final morning's Leadership Scholar breakfast for seminary students. Again, the overwhelming majority of us were white and being waited on by what must have been an almost one hundred percent Hispanic workforce. Hispanic waiters and waitresses were constantly coming to our tables offering coffee, orange juice, more water, or more coffee, or to take our plates.

Fellow students from numerous CBF-affiliated seminaries and I were talking at the table—trying to envision ourselves as peacemakers and justice seekers in the midst of such luxury—when a waiter leaned over my shoulder and offered to pour me some coffee.

I looked up to say "no thanks" and to apologize for our spoiled arrogance; it actually crossed my mind to get up, let him sit in my seat, pour him some coffee, and go get him some breakfast.

But when I looked up, I could not speak. I heard in the most clearly audible voice—though he was saying nothing—"I came not to be served but to serve. I'd like to pour you some coffee."

I said nothing as I held out my fine coffee cup. At my eye level was the waiter's name tag pinned to his chest: J-e-s-u-s.

And I heard the voice again: "I came not to be served but to serve. Just shut up and let me serve you today, Bert." Jesus was right in front of me, and I didn't recognize him. If not for the name tag . . .

I was too caught up in my own agenda—in Christ's name, of course—to have ever noticed. I was meeting him face to face, and I didn't recognize Jesus.

A biblical story that fascinates me is the one where some guys are walking along the road to Emmaus after the resurrection; these were guys who knew Jesus personally. And there is Jesus walking with them and talking with them, but they don't even recognize him. He's a total stranger to them.

Until . . . they invite this stranger into their house.

Until . . . they invite the stranger to sit at their table and share a meal.

Until . . . the stranger takes over and breaks the bread and gives thanks.

The stranger being welcomed and served becomes the one to take what is present and serve those who are present with him. *Then* their eyes are opened, and *then* they know that Jesus is with them.

Thanks to the Johnny Cash Flower-Pickin' Festival, I shook the hand of Marshall Grant, the hand that managed Johnny Cash and the hand that managed the Statler Brothers, whose song is one of the most simplistically profound expressions of the gospel:

Would you recognize Jesus if you met him face to face
or would you wonder if He's just someone you couldn't place?
You may not find Him coming in a chariot of the Lord
Jesus could be riding in a '49 Ford.

Notes

1. If the Statler Brothers had a following like that of the Grateful Dead, then my parents were "Statler Heads." My family traveled all over the state of Louisiana, up to Staunton, Virginia, and to several places in between to see the Statlers in concert. Mom was a member of "The Class of '57" (that's pretty important—just ask any Statler Brothers fan).

2. The only two actual brothers in the Statler Brothers, Don and Harold Reid, wrote "Would You Recognize Jesus?" and included it on the Statler Brothers 1976 album Harold, Lew, Phil, & Don. Johnny Cash—their longtime friend and their one-time boss—also recorded it.

The Burden of Belief

(Ode to Doubt and Daniel Bailey)

This reflection is inspired by the song "Burden of Belief" by Daniel Bailey and by the Gospel of John.

"My Lord and my God!" Thomas exclaimed. Then Jesus told him, "You believe because you have seen me. Blessed are those who believe without seeing me" (John 20:19-29, NLT).

Some of us find it easy to believe.
    We are strong, firm, resilient, and certain in our faith.
    Some of us just know that Jesus is alive.
        That Jesus is Lord.
        That God is in control.

And blessed are you who believe without seeing!

But then there are some of us
    who work very hard
    to convince ourselves that we believe.
We're scared of potential consequences
    of admitting we have any doubts.

We've heard it said too many times . . .
    if you believe;
    if you pray;
    if you ask;
    if your faith is strong enough.

And we want God to love us.
  We need Jesus to save us.
  We want the Lord to heal us.
  But we're afraid we may not be sincere enough to satisfy God.

We view God like we see Tinker Bell . . .
  we must clap and proclaim convincingly
  that we do believe in fairies!
  That we do believe in Jesus!
  That we do believe in the Resurrection!
  That we do believe in God!

And we work
  and work
  and work
  so that we can hope to hear these words:
  "Blessed are YOU who believed without seeing me."

But there are also some of us who find it very difficult to believe . . .
  when we have seen the unspeakable brutality of the Holocaust;
  when we have seen the unspeakable brutality of racism;
  when we have felt the burning sting of the whip from
      "Christian" men;
  when we have watched an innocent child suffer mercilessly from
      birth;
  when we watched a mother bury her own child;
  when we have been betrayed by those we love and trust the most.

And we can look around us and say
  "blessed are you who believe
  but we have seen . . .
  but we have seen . . .
  we have seen too much . . .

And we're not about to play
  silly Tinker Bell games

to massage the ego
   of some god suffering from low self-esteem.

Yes, blessed are you who believe and have not seen . . .

But we have seen, oh yes,
   and nobody knows
   the horrors we've seen . . .

and believing is really, really hard work.

Reverend Jim England tells of speaking with a fellow minister/friend
   who had just gone through the death of two close family members,
   one under very tragic circumstances.

The minister/friend shared with Reverend England
   that she honestly did not know
   if she even believes this stuff about God anymore.

And Jim replied to her,
   that Sunday is coming around.
   What will she—a minister—do?

And she answered,
   "I guess I have to trust [the congregation]
   to believe for me
   until I can believe it again for myself."

Sometimes our doubts are so great—
   and sometimes we cannot believe anymore.

But we want to believe,
   and we keep coming to worship,
   we keep talking about faith with trusted friends,
   and we keep singing together,

and we discover that even when we don't believe anymore,
    our congregation is believing for us,
    is trusting for us,
    is sustaining our faith for us,
    until we are able to believe again ourselves.

All of us have various degrees of certainty about God;
    about Jesus;
    about hope;
    about life eternal;
    about abundant life now.

But it's not about you convincing yourself that you have no doubts
    in order to convince God that you believe enough
    (whatever "enough" is).

It's about God loving you regardless of your ability to believe.

And it's about the community of faith carrying our faith for us.

Feel the breath of Jesus breathing upon you and hear the voice of Jesus saying, "Peace be with you. As the Father has sent me, so I am sending you."

So let it be.

Everybody Hurts

(Ode to Michael and R.E.M.)

As soon as the news hit that rock band R.E.M. was retiring after over thirty years together, a call went out to writers to compose tributes to favorite R.E.M. songs. I can't say I've been a fan of the original band—Michael Stipe, Bill Berry, Mike Mills, and Peter Buck—for all those thirty years, but I can say I've been a fan for the last twenty-five or twenty-six.

I immediately replied with my request to write about their song "Everybody Hurts." Actually, "request to write about" can be interpreted in this context to mean "begged, pleaded, and may have crossed the line over to 'demanding.'" (It's a very personal song for me.) The nod of approval came my way, and off I went.

I should've asked for "Stand"—something peppy and fun—or maybe something from *Reconstruction of the Fables*. "Everybody Hurts" is just too personal.

I have a small, select group of friends (more like brothers) who pray for each other, encourage each other, and carry each other. We are forever bonded together because of our connections with the deepest, darkest depression, and with suicide.

"Take comfort in your friends," sings Mr. Stipe . . . little does he know. Or perhaps he does.

When your day is long and your night . . . your night is yours alone;
When you're sure you've had enough of this life . . . hang on.

Michael (not Stipe, but a different one) was one of the friends in our group. He was a gifted and beloved minister. I was just getting to know him (I was the new kid in this circle of angst-ridden ministers/writers). An online private discussion about depression and faith emerged within our small group. Someone mentioned Elijah's depression and Elijah crawling inside the cave to die. Michael posted, "Yes, but Elijah's story had a happy ending."

Just a few days later, Michael's wife came home and found him—not hanging on but just . . . hanging.

Despite our best efforts, there was no comfort for Michael, not even in his friends.

Sometimes everything is wrong . . . .
If you feel like letting go, hold on . . . .

For me, more than any other song, "Everybody Hurts" gets it. The words are repetitive and direct, yet they overflow with the imagery of overwhelming darkness. The music, at first, is simple, slow, and hypnotizing.

Stipe doesn't preach. He just shares the emotions as only one who has experienced them personally can. (I have no idea about his experiences with depression, but somehow he *knows*.) He doesn't smile and try to make anyone be a shiny, happy person. He simply shares in the emotions. And instead of offering easy answers or "always look on the bright side" platitudes, he just pleads.

When you think you've had too much of this life, hang on . . . .

The music begins to build. The strings begin lifting the music higher. The passion grows stronger. The pleas and the rhythm build on each other until musically it borders on gospel (especially with the organ). Somehow Stipe's continuing plea to "hold on" becomes a chant of hope.

Hold on . . . hooooold onnnn

For others of us in our small group of close-knit friends, we've each pleaded with each other many a long, dark night.

Hold on.

Sometimes only those who have been there can understand the depths of the loneliness, and only those who understand have earned the right to say, "Hold on."

Take comfort in your friends . . . .

R.E.M.'s "Everybody Hurts" is more than a song. It is itself a dear, close, comforting friend.

For Michael (not Stipe, but the other one), I wish we could have helped you hold on a little longer. And for Michael (Stipe), Bill (Berry), Peter (Buck), and Mike (Mills)—thanks be to God.

Of Jesus, the Chattahoochee, and *Taxi Driver*

(or, There's Dung in the Baptismal Waters)

Jesus was dipped by John in the Chattahoochee. That's how Clarence Jordan's *Cotton Patch Gospels* share the story of Jesus' baptism.

I wish I knew Alan Jackson; I would've asked him to come over to church and read Scripture. Imagine Alan Jackson, who sings about the Chattahoochee, reading in his wonderful southern-Georgia drawl the southern-country telling of Jesus' baptism in the Chattahoochee!

But I don't know Alan Jackson, so on a whim I emailed a friend of mine who also grew up along the Chattahoochee and has a great southern-Georgia drawl, and she readily agreed to read our Scripture story—all the way from her home in Oregon. And, with a word of greeting to us, and with the word of God for us, author Karen Spears Zacharias (via the magic of video and the Internet) shared with my congregation the Cotton Patch version of Jesus' baptism.

I spent a good part of the week preparing for my sermon by reflecting on the baptism scene from the film *O Brother, Where Art Thou?* Delmar jumps into the river along with a robed congregation, cuts in line, and has all his sins washed away at the preacher's hand (including that Piggly Wiggly he knocked over in Yazoo). "Come on in, boys, the water is fine!"

What a great scene of hope and redemption and good ol' old-time religion in the rural American South.

That is, until the news during the day that Saturday distracted me from *O Brother, Where Art Thou?* and made me think instead of Robert De Niro as Travis Bickle in *Taxi Driver*, a movie that is not conducive to meditating on Jesus and baptism. But maybe it should be.

36   OF MICE AND MINISTERS

On January 8, 2011, Arizona Congresswoman Gabrielle Giffords was shot in the head (though she survived) by an angry man whose gunfire outside a grocery store political event not only nearly killed a congresswoman but did kill a federal judge and a handful of others, and wounded several more.

How could we speak on Sunday about the baptism of Jesus amid the reality of the hatred, fear, violence, and assassinations that had erupted on Saturday in Arizona?

Churches have such beautiful and glorious painted images of Jesus being baptized—the pure white light shining down from heaven like an upside-down triangle with the point at the dove on Jesus' head. It's such a reverent and majestic moment in time.

But Jesus' baptism did not happen in some holy, purified, unstained-by-human-sin river.

Nope. If we would read the Gospel of Matthew like we do our favorite Stephen King novels, instead of in segments and one-verse-at-a-time-Sweet-Jesus, we would experience Joseph and Mary fleeing with Jesus to Egypt to escape the wrath of a jealous king. They return after Herod's death, and then BAM! There's John in the river baptizing folks, and here comes Jesus. About thirty years later in less than a few sentences, and with the bitter taste of a turbulent society still fresh in our mouths, we are reading about Jesus wading into the water.

Reading Matthew from the *Cotton Patch Gospels* is even more revealing; Clarence Jordan tells the story of Jesus not in and around Jerusalem and under Roman rule, but in and around Atlanta and Birmingham, all under Jim Crow rule—translating New Testament Greek into the southern dialect of the civil-rights era American South.

Jordan forces us to consider the reality of the gospel story in the midst of our very real American world of political hatred, racism, fear, murder, burning crosses, assassinations, cell phones, Internet access, instant news, and individuals and fringe groups feeding off the heated rhetoric calling for revolutions. Far from being simply a glorious, wonderful, beautiful day at the river as portrayed in our paintings, the baptism of Jesus happens in *our* world—with civil unrest, mayhem, inequalities of wealth and power, and assassinations of presidents, leaders, judges, and even innocent children.

I've never been swimming in the Chattahoochee River, but I have been swimming in creeks and ponds. And at five or six years of age, I clearly remember my older cousin instructing me that, unlike the clean and chlorinated swimming pools I was used to in Metairie, Louisiana, when swimming in a country pond with fish and cows, you don't have to get out of the water to "use the bathroom" because there is no bathroom to use—you just "let it go" while you're standing in the water.

Baptismal waters today are clear and heated, filling what look like nice, big bathtubs. After all, we preach cleansing and washing away sins as part of the baptism symbolism. But Jesus was baptized in waters that could wash away dirt as well as expose you to animal excrement and everything else that finds its way into a river in the wild.

And that is exactly why Jesus' baptism is so important in the face of violent events in Arizona. This is exactly what ties the innocence of Delmar in *O Brother, Where Art Thou?* to the alienation and anger of Travis Bickle in *Taxi Driver.*

Not only does Matthew put Jesus' baptism directly in the context of Herod and the threat of a new king, but the very act itself mystically involves the dung of the world simultaneously washing over Jesus in the purifying act of baptism. Jesus' baptism reminds us that our faith is not one of escape from the world or one of victorious rule over the world, but of loving service to the world just as it is.

The disturbing reality of assassinations and the joyous old-time baptismal gatherings at the river . . .

Jesus going under and coming up from the Chattahoochee . . .

For God so loved the world, indeed!

Now then, I wonder if Karen Spears Zacharias knows Alan Jackson.

Of Mice and Ministers

(Ode to Advent and Axl Rose)

I've heard it said that Axl Rose, front man of Guns N' Roses, was and maybe still is an angry, angry man. I have no reason to doubt it. There simply is no denying that Guns N' Roses exploded into the nation's consciousness in late 1987, and for the next five to six years, until their implosion in 1993, they were one of the most important, exciting, terrifyingly self-destructive, and unpredictable rock and roll band ever.

Guns N' Roses have been on my mind a lot recently, and for an obvious reason—we Christians are celebrating the season of Advent. And honestly, nothing says "Advent" and "Incarnation" better than Guns N' Roses uncensored and at high volume. Don't believe me? Just listen to what should be the international anthem of Advent, "Welcome to the Jungle."[1]

This epiphany occurred to me during a recent stay at an inexpensive motel chain in a small city. To save money, and because I'm a sucker for Tom Bodet's voice, I reserved a room online with the motel chain; I did not see the location of said motel or view any pictures to tell if it was a well-kept establishment.

Because the Mississippi State University semester was winding down and all that was left were final exams, at one o'clock in the morning I was sitting up in the bed with my MacBook in my lap, calculating attendance grades and semester averages, when I saw an uninvited visitor walk right into my room.

The door was bolted and locked, of course, but being the cheapest motel in town—this side of getting a run-down Norman Bates-style room—there was at least a three-quarter-inch gap where the bottom of the door was supposed to meet the floor. The guest, who just strolled on in as if it was his house, was a rather large mouse.

He stopped in the middle of the floor and looked and me. I looked at him. Then he continued coming toward the bed and disappeared. Disappeared under (or into?) the bed.

I couldn't find him, and I never saw him again. But I did notice a few openings in the box springs and in the wall behind the bed indicating that this could be his home and *I* was the unwelcomed company.

I almost called the front desk, but what good would that do? I paid $33 for a room at an old, run-down motel; a motel with a questionable nightclub right behind it; a motel that left its light on for all God's living creatures. Should I have expected the Memphis Peabody?

I noticed that the people outside my room (between 1:00 and 3:00 a.m. there were a lot of people outside my room, and there was a lot of activity going on) had that hard, wear-and-tear look about them caused by years of hard laboring and/or hard living. And many seemed to be laboring pretty hard that night to make a little extra cash in some not-so-admirable ways.

Here I was, worried about a little mouse in my room. (Though, again, it was a rather *big* mouse.) At that moment, I wished I had coughed up the extra dough for a nicer, middle-class hotel room. Clean. Comfortable. And typically mouse-free (or at least the mice are kind enough to stay inside the walls, thus "out of sight, out of mind").

Many of us grew up in and assumed a middle-class image of Christian faith. It's comfortable. It's nice and cozy and familiar. It's organized, neat, presentable, respectable, and relatively mouse-free (or at least, everything is kept "out of sight" and therefore "out of mind").

Advent, though, forces us to acknowledge that there's nothing comfortable or nice or cozy or organized or neat or respectable about the coming of our Lord. It's dangerous. It's dirty. It's smelly. And mice roam freely.

It occurs among people who live hard lives and who work hard, unglorified jobs (sometimes in less-than-legal ways), and they have the visible scars, stains, anger, and pain to show for it.

It's into this real and harsh world—which many of us in the church wish we could keep out of our sight and out of our minds—that the

Christ child is born. Why? Because it's the real world filled with the real people whom God so loves.

This Advent season, as I welcome the Christ child, I can't stop hearing Axl's angry and threatening greeting from a world I'd rather pretend doesn't exist: "Welcome to the jungle; watch it bring you to your knees; I want to watch you bleed!"

And by the grace of our Lord Jesus Christ, may the church be as committed to living among and loving the real people in the real world as is the God we proclaim to serve.

I wonder if Axl is free to sing in church this Sunday . . . .

Note

1. The song appears on the band's 1987 album, *Appetite for Destruction.*

Harry Potter and the Incarnate Christ

I love great fantasy/adventure tales, especially ones in which ordinary people in ordinary places find an escape, or rather a hidden entrance, into another world where anything is possible.

In the Harry Potter stories—my personal favorites—children run through a brick wall in a London train station, between platforms 9 and 10 (platform 9¾ to be exact) and begin their journey to Hogwarts, a world filled with mystery, magic, and life-and-death battles between love . . . and power.

This Advent season, there's another grand story of adventure and mystery being told. But it's a little different. In this other story, no one escapes from our world into some other realm.

Instead, some other realm breaks into and takes up residence here in the normal, ordinary, real world in which we live. The Eternal One breaks into our time and space, takes on our flesh and blood, and brings adventure and life to us.

Mary, a young teenage girl, has just been informed by her father of her upcoming marriage to some man named Joseph, a carpenter, and she is trying to digest this information. After all, she sort of had her eyes set on Hezekiah—that freewheeling bohemian boy down the street who plays folk music on the lyre.

But that's not the way life is: everyone knows parents arrange for you to marry some man you've probably never even met before. Some things will never change.

So Mary sighs deeply, kisses her parents goodnight, and goes to the kitchen to grab a Moon Pie and RC Cola. Then she settles in on the couch to watch reruns of *I Love Lucy* on late-night TV.

All the lights are off, leaving only the glow from the TV screen, and all of a sudden, right there in front of her face, appearing out of nowhere, is some sort of man—a strange man if he's even human at all!

Mary chokes briefly on her RC and sits up straight in shock, unable to find her voice. She's trying to yell for her dad, but nothing is coming out.

Then this glowing, radiant being speaks: "Hello, you blessed one! THE LORD IS WITH YOU!" This thing tells her she's going to become pregnant, give birth to a baby boy, and name him Jesus. Oh, and Jesus will rule forever.

There's stunned silence for a moment. Mary begins looking around suspiciously to see if this is some kind of prank. She finds no strings, no mirrors, no projector, no other people around.

She reaches out to touch this being . . . this messenger . . . this angel? And she falls back onto the couch and yells, "That's impossible! I ain't even married yet!"[1]

The angelic being explains about the Holy Spirit passing over her, and that her child will be called "God's Son." Nothing, you see, is impossible with God! And Mary, overwhelmed but aware that she is in the presence of a messenger from God, sighs and says, "Alrighty then, I am the Lord's servant. So let it be."

And in a flash, the messenger is gone, leaving Mary alone again with her RC and Moon Pie and *I Love Lucy* on TV.

The adventure begins—right here in *this* world: the real world of jobs, families, dirty diapers, schools, bills, taxes, governments, crooks, betrayals, birth and death, diseases and so on. For Mary, this adventure means being cast in a highly suspicious role as an unmarried pregnant girl and then as the mother of a child who grows up to be executed as a criminal.

We too often approach Christmas like we approach movies—as a beautiful story to be retold and enjoyed year after year—but then the story ends and we walk out of the theater (oops! I mean the sanctuary) and return to our ordinary lives in the real world.

Maybe if we spend a little less time waiting for Jesus to come and take us out of this world and a little more time looking for the Incarnate Christ living in our world, the Christmas story will cease to be merely a feel-good, illuminated, cheap plastic lawn decoration and become a life-changing adventure as an agent of God's grace in a world sorely needing it.

It's the adventure of loving the world as God so loves the world. It's the adventure of loving the people God so loves. Like Mary before us, it's actively participating with God in this great adventure filled with holy mystery and life-and-death battles between love . . . and power.

Note

1. Back then, young girls weren't sent to school to learn proper English.

Of Janis Joplin and Christian Women

(Ode to Being Unladylike)

I was three years old the first time I heard Janis Joplin's "Mercedes Benz" on the radio. In 1971, Dad (though not a fan of rock and roll) thought the song was quite funny, and we heard it several times during a family trip that year. Forty years later, Janis Joplin remains one of my favorite female singers. Scratch that, she's one of my favorite singers of all time *period.*

Janis sure wrestled with her pain and her demons, a fight she soon lost in this world. But she was incredibly gifted, too. One of her greatest gifts was that she refused to conform; she played by her own rules; and she risked being unladylike in order to make the music God placed within her.

One of the most inspiring and challenging preachers I have ever heard is also a dear family friend—Reverend Karen Thomas Smith. That's right: her name is Karen. The daughter of a Baptist preacher man, in the mid-1980s Karen attended a Baptist college and then went on to a non-Baptist divinity school to prepare for the ministry. Karen grew up in a denomination that was fighting internally at the time about the "proper place" of women; today, she is among the growing ranks of female clergy who dare to know that "their place" is wherever God leads them (for the record, like her dad, she's a Baptist preacher).

One of Karen's greatest gifts (and she is very gifted in many ways) is her stubborn determination not to be confined by social expectations. Even today, she risks being seen as unladylike—both in America and around the world—because of her openness to the Holy Spirit.

Pam Hogeweide is a "virtual" friend, a writing colleague, and author of the book *Unladylike: Resisting the Injustice of Inequality in the Church*.[1] Pam is sort of a mixture of Karen Thomas Smith and Janis Joplin. Her multicolored, tattooed arms and her style of dress suggest that she'd fit right in at the Bonnaroo Music and Arts Festival, but not so much at First Respectable Church of Anytown. Yet the preacher-like conviction with which she writes reveals an intimate relationship with Christ and with our Holy Scriptures.

Being unladylike is Pam's wrestling match with a largely male-dominated Christendom in which women still have "their place" ("polite oppression," Pam calls it). With stories, humor, research, and a Spirit-led, biblical passion for justice, Pam celebrates women who dared to play by a different set of rules within the patriarchal church, and she challenges women and men together to follow the way of Jesus, which tends to buck convention and tradition.

If you're looking for a good resource for a small-group study on the role of women in the church, or if you're working through this issue yourself and want to read a great book on the subject, be sure to get a copy of Pam Hogeweide's *Unladylike*.

If you're looking for a Baptist preacher to fill your pulpit one Sunday, I can connect you with Karen Thomas Smith (note, though, that her schedule tends to be quite full—most of the year she's pastoring outside the United States).

And if you're looking for an incredible, soul-filled, bluesy voice, you can't go wrong with Janis Joplin.

But if you are looking for God's work in the world to be limited to a private club for men, then you are in for a big surprise. For brave, unladylike women everywhere—thanks be to God!

Note

1. Pam Hogeweide, *Unladylike: Resisting the Injustice of Inequality in the Church* (Folsom CA: Civitas Press, 2012).

Of Blisters and Ashes, High Heels and Lent

Love God; love yourself as God loves you; and love others as you love yourself.

As a Baptist minister, Ash Wednesday and the Christian season of Lent are unfamiliar to me. But as I have tried to understand and embrace them, I have come to believe that Ash Wednesday and Lent are designed to do nothing less than to help us love God, love ourselves as God loves us, and love others as we love ourselves.

One Monday just prior to Ash Wednesday, I participated in the "Walk a Mile in Her Shoes" event at Mississippi State University. Men—students, faculty, and community leaders—donned high heels, slippers, pumps, etc., to draw attention to and stop sexual assault, rape, and violence against women.

Then Tuesday morning arrived, and I became aware of several blisters on my toes and on the bottoms of my feet. My ankles hurt. My knees hurt. My wife told me that she was proud of me for doing the walk, and she was sorry I was hurting.

But as I was putting bandages on my sores, my thoughts turned to the deep hurt and unspeakable pain experienced by a college friend who was raped; my thoughts turned to a coworker who, as a young girl, was sexually molested by a trusted family friend; and my thoughts turned to the fact that when I look out over the students in my classes, I will be looking out upon several young women who, while being at college, have experienced sexual aggression and violence—and perhaps I will even be looking out upon some of the young men who have committed those acts.

In the days since walking that mile in women's shoes, with each pinch of pain that comes with each step, I've noticed that I am praying for the women I know whose pain is deeper and far more severe than my blisters and aches will ever be. A few blisters and sore ankles created a level of empathy for others I had not had before.

I often show a documentary on Islam to my Introduction to Religion classes. In it, a Muslim man talks about Ramadan—the Islamic month of fasting. He speaks of this as a time to learn patience, humility, and spirituality; a time to focus on God and prayer; a time to ask forgiveness for sins, to pray for guidance, and to take steps toward developing self-restraint.

He talks about Ramadan and fasting in the larger context of the Five Pillars of Islam, which includes almsgiving (or charity). The man says that for almsgiving to be pure, it should not be simply done out of guilt or obligation, but out of genuine empathetic concern for others. He suggests that to be empathetic with someone who is hungry, he must first know the pangs of hunger. Thus, the month of fasting helps this man focus on his sins, his repentance, and his need for God, but it also forms within him a physical connection with those who hurt and suffer throughout the year.

Being a Baptist, I'm still quite new to the rich Christian traditions of Ash Wednesday and Lent. I do know, though, that it's more than just "giving up" something or trying to "pick up" something else. Jesus doesn't speak of Lent (obviously, it developed later in the church), but he does tell us that everything comes down to loving God and loving others as you love yourself.

So, whatever Lent is, it certainly has to be a means to the end of helping us love God. And with all of the "giving up" and "taking on" and fasting and discipline and confession and repentance, it also has to be a means of helping us love ourselves as God loves us.

And maybe it is also a means of helping us love others, too.

Maybe in our humble confessions beginning with Ash Wednesday, when we remind ourselves that each of us comes from dust and to dust each of us shall return, maybe in whatever we will do (or not do) during the season of Lent that helps us love God with all of our heart, soul, mind, and strength and helps us love ourselves as God loves us—maybe in all of this, God will also grow within us a greater sense of empathy for others.

It could be that in some self-denial, and even with a little pain, God draws our attention to the pain and needs of others.

You may not have blisters on your feet, but many of us have had ashes smudged on our foreheads. At the very least, may God take the ashes from our foreheads and place them in our vision so that everyone we see has the cross of ashes on their foreheads, reminding us that they, just like us, come from ashes, and to ashes we will all return.

And may God use whatever discipline you may practice to nurture a greater sense of empathy for a neighbor, a friend, a stranger, an enemy.

Love God. Love yourself. Love others. This is the purpose of Lent.

Now, if you'll excuse me, I still have some blisters to tend to.

O Jesus, Where Art Thou?

Easter Sunday.

Had it occurred in Depression-Era Mississippi, rather than in first-century Roman-occupied Jerusalem (and it very well could have), when the women arrived at the tomb they would have beheld a man dressed in a long white robe, whittling away on a stick, who likely would have said something like this: "You lookin' for Jesus, of Natchez. But he ain't here. He up'n run oft!"[1]

All four Gospel writers tell the Easter story (as we now refer to it) differently. If we try to put the four accounts together like puzzle pieces to make one complete picture, we may get confused and frustrated—the pieces just don't fit together.

It did begin so early in the morning that it was still dark. The stone had been moved, rolled away, leaving the tomb open.

One Gospel says there was an earthquake.

Were there two figures dressed in white at the tomb, or just one?

How many women went to the tomb? Which women were at the tomb?

Was Peter there? Any of the other disciples?

Did Jesus appear at the tomb? To whom did Jesus first appear? What did he say?

Read just one Gospel, and you'll get solid answers to some of these questions. Read each of the four Gospels, and you'll likely give up trying to make sense of it all. And that's probably because, like life itself, these events simply do not make sense.

Frederick Buechner writes, "When it comes to just what happened, there can be no certainty. That something unimaginable happened, there can be no doubt. The symbol of Easter is the empty tomb."[2]

Mississippi Baptist preacher Will D. Campbell wrote a novel some years back titled *The Glad River*.[3] The protagonist, a fictional, small-town Mississippi man, goes by the name "Doops."

Doops was born and raised in the local small-town Baptist church, but he refused to get baptized and never joined any church. That's not because he didn't believe in Jesus but because in fact he *did* believe.

One Easter Sunday, Doops gets drunk and walks into the local Baptist church in which he was raised—right in the middle of the preacher delivering the Easter sermon. Doops interrupts the preacher and disrupts the sermon, yelling out, "He is NOT here! He is RISEN!"

Then Doops runs out and goes to the other churches in town—Methodist, Presbyterian, Holiness, and so on—yelling out in each of them, "HE AIN'T HERE! HE DONE GOT UP AND RUN OFF!"

Doops sounds like one of the Old Testament prophets, the way he runs in and out of churches implying that the pretty buildings and orderly worship services and confident preachers in their new Easter suits are themselves the very tombs that cannot hold the Body of Christ today.

The story of the empty tomb reminds us that the Body of Christ is *not* confined by buildings or by doctrines and teachings.

The story of the empty tomb reminds us that, even on those occasional Sundays when we go to a church service needing to see Jesus but do not find him, if we listen, we may hear those words spoken to the women at the tomb: "Don't be scared. Jesus ain't here. He up'n run oft!"

And that is *not* necessarily a condemnation of the church as Doops intended it to be. It may just be the hope we need: that the Christ who lives is on the move; that the Christ who lives is alive in the world around us; that while we celebrate the resurrection inside our churches, the Body of Christ is alive and well and walking outside our walls.

O Jesus, where art thou?

A band called The Lost Dogs tells us simply to try looking where Jesus told us he would be:

That's Jesus in the homeless faces;
with the junkies in their livin' hell;

that's Jesus with the drunks and in the lonely places—
the rest home and prison cells.
That's where Jesus is, where we ought to be;
here's where Jesus works, inside you and me;
with the folks with AIDS, and the suffering kids . . .
that's where Jesus lives.[4]

Christians around the world attend church services every Easter Sunday to celebrate the resurrection. And that's good.

Now may we follow our risen Lord out of our protected, locked enclosures and back out into the world where it's dangerous and dirty, where the lonely and suffering and hurting folks are . . . for *that* is where Jesus is.

Notes

1. That's a paraphrase, of course, from Mark's Gospel.

2. See "Easter" in Buechner's *Whistling in the Dark: A Doubter's Dictionary* (San Francisco: HarperSanFrancisco, 1993) 46.

3. *The Glad River* is one of my all-time favorites among all my favorite books. When you finish this book, go buy *The Glad River* (Macon: Smyth & Helwys, 2011).

4. "That's Where Jesus Is" was written by Terry Scott Taylor of the Lost Dogs and recorded on their 2006 album, *The Lost Cabin and the Mystery Trees*.

A Kiss of Solidarity

(or, When a Picture Is Worth Far More than Thousands and Thousands of Words)

A picture is worth a thousand words, they say. This week, I learned just how true that is.

I've written thousands of words over the past several years about how the church has failed our gay and lesbian family members, friends, and neighbors, and why I, as a minister of the gospel, seek to welcome, affirm, and fully include everyone both in the church and in civic life. Not only are my words written for all to see; I have also spoken such messages to groups, on panels, and from pulpits. Thousands and thousands of words.

But when I recently asked a friend not to publicly post a picture of a Christian brother and me goofing off in which he puckered up and I leaned in and kissed him on his cheek, I had no idea how hurtful my request would be.

In the context of a fun evening at a church fellowship, when people were posing for pictures, someone snapped the photo in question. Later, I asked the photographer to please not post the photo of "the kiss"; my reasoning was that, while it was quite funny to us, it might not be good for public viewing (me being the pastor and all). I figured that people outside of that evening who didn't know the context would criticize not only me as a pastor but also the church and people in the church. My motive was to protect everyone; after all, it was just silly fun, anyway.

Though I didn't know it, the picture had already been posted. After my friend received my request, she immediately deleted the photo. A few days later, I learned how important that picture was to some friends of mine. What was done in the spirit of fun on the spur of the moment, it seems, had significant meaning to others. My credibility increased as a minister among my friends in the LGBTQ[1] community because, to quote one of the comments I received, "It was awesome that a straight pastor would be cool enough to jokingly have kissed another guy."

When the photo disappeared and inquiring minds discovered that I had requested it not be posted, my credibility sunk. The impression my action gave was that I was afraid of "looking gay."

One friend wrote to me, "It feels like someone thought there was something inherently wrong with the photo . . . ." He meant that it is one thing for me to say it's okay to be gay, but that doesn't mean much if I'm not secure enough not to worry about people thinking I am gay.

Another friend wrote to me, "I think it would be good for people to know how these things can harm. I know it's something that most people in the Church wouldn't understand, but the fact is most people in the Church have never felt physically unsafe because of the way they look. Most people in the Church have never been harassed in a bathroom. Most people in the Church have never spent more time on a date looking over their shoulder than enjoying their date. And I think it is important for straight people to understand that what they might think is a bad thing can actually make others feel safe, even if it's something small like a silly photo."

That last sentence is the one the hit me the hardest. "It is important for straight people to understand that what they might think is a bad thing can actually make others feel safe, even if it's something small like a silly photo."

I've always liked to think of myself as an advocate for and an ally of those on the margins, as a person willing to stand in solidarity with anyone feeling left out, especially with those being forced out and treated unequally and unjustly. It's at the core of my faith—that as Jesus identified himself with the outcasts, so should we as Jesus' followers.

A simple request not to post a photo showed me how so far I am from reflecting the good news of Christ in my actions. All my thousands of words don't mean a thing if my actions keep me distanced from others, if my actions show my solidarity with the status quo rather than with those who strive for equality.

Scott Lipsey on left, Bert on right. (Photo credit: Melissa Grimes)

So here's the photo. Nothing special, nothing serious, nothing but simple, light-hearted fun. But for my LGBTQ friends, neighbors, and members of my congregation, it's worth far, far more than even ten thousand words of support. It represents solidarity.

Besides, Scott and I were just doing what the Apostle Paul frequently instructed us all to do, anyway: greeting each other with a holy kiss.

Note

1. L (lesbian), G (gay), B (bisexual), T (transgender), and Q (questioning/queer).

The Church and the New Civil Rights Movement

(Owed to Dick Brogan)

Richard "Dick" Brogan was a personal friend, and he was one of my heroes.

Dick was a white Mississippi Baptist minister who worked tirelessly to build relationships between whites and blacks during segregation and even up until he passed away in 2011. Not so long ago, Dick was followed, harassed, threatened, and derided as a "nigger lover" because he not only dared to speak against segregation but also dared to act as if, in Christ, there really is no Jew or Greek and no black or white.

Shortly before he died, Dick, a veteran of the civil rights movement, said that gay rights is today's gospel movement. I believe he was right.

Consider the role of black churches in leading the civil rights movement and the role of white churches in resisting it. (By the way, isn't anyone disturbed that we still have "black churches" and "white churches"?)

Though Martin Luther King, Jr., and other black ministers found liberation and hope in the Bible, some white preachers remained silent while many others openly preached segregation and racial inequality as biblically sound.

"Red birds do not fly with blue birds," white Christians smugly joked, emphasizing, "It's just the natural order of things."

With a clear conscience, white church deacons and Sunday school teachers witnessed (and some participated in) lynchings, cross burnings, bombings, and mob violence against marchers and sit-in participants. Stories abound in Mississippi of deacons at white churches armed with guns, protecting the dignity of worship for the white folks within. They were, after all, defending "the way God intended things to be." Black people were tolerated just fine as long as "they stayed in their place."

A Broadman Bible Commentary from 1970 argues that the historical context of John 3—the story of Nicodemus and Jesus—needs to be seen and understood beyond a simple meeting of two individuals.[1] Instead, we should view it as Jesus, "the leader of a dynamic renewal movement within Judaism pleading with Nicodemus as a guardian of the religious establishment to open the life of Israel to the power of the Spirit already at work in their midst."[2] Furthermore, the author of that commentary reminds us that "The people of God are called to renewal in each successive era of their existence."[3]

In the 1950s and 1960s, Baptist preachers like Martin Luther King, Jr., and Dick Brogan followed the leadership of the Holy Spirit and called the people of God to renewal in a new era of their existence. Through them, God was transforming the religious life of people, often meeting the greatest resistance through the "guardians" of the truth and the faith.

Again, Jesus pleaded with the religious establishment of his day, according to the Broadman Commentary, to "open the life of Israel to the power of the work of the Holy Spirit . . . ."

The larger religious community's response to Jesus was his crucifixion.

And so King, Brogan, and others made the same plea. The responses to them were death threats, violence, exile, and, for King, assassination.

We are in the midst of another renewal. We are in the midst of another set of leaders pleading with the guardians of the Christian establishment to open the life of the church to the power of the Holy Spirit already at work, and some of the same words are being exchanged. Variations of the same expressions of hatred are emerging in response.

There are a growing number of "gay churches" and welcoming and affirming groups pleading with the larger Christian community to recognize the movement of the Holy Spirit among the LGBTQ community. And many of the long-standing institutionalized "straight churches" are actively resisting the work of God among those whom the "religious guardians" insist are not worthy. (Let's hope that our grandchildren will not one day sigh and ask us why there have to be "gay churches" and "straight churches.")

"They want their children to go to school with our children! They want to live in the neighborhood we live in! They want the same rights we have!"

"God created Adam and Eve, not Adam and Steve. It's just the natural order of things."

And with clear consciences, good churchgoers openly bully, harass, and tease their gay neighbors—trying to get the gays back in the closet ("to keep them in their place").

Despite what almost every single church sign says, openly LGBTQ people are *not* welcomed in most churches across the South and across America. There may not be deacons armed with guns to keep them out and to protect the "dignity" of the worship service for the righteous folks within, but Sunday school lessons, book studies, and sermons bully them either to stay in the closet or stay out of the church.

When bullying leads to suicide, the church at large—at best—sits in silence. At worst, it leads the attack. Too many Baptist pastors are pressured to stay quiet on the issue, while other Baptist pastors continue to verbally terrorize LGBTQ people sitting quietly in their pews, living quietly in their families, and working quietly in their communities.

I am sometimes asked why I continue to write and speak about being a gay-friendly Baptist minister. Then a fellow pastor answers for me by making national news when he acts like a 1950s Southern governor justifying racial segregation (not so long ago, a brother in North Carolina preached what some called a "beat-the-gay-away" sermon—instructing parents how to deal with boys and girls who may not be masculine enough or feminine enough, respectfully).

But, like Dick Brogan, deep in my heart I do believe that blacks and whites and gays and straights will walk hand in hand someday.

Notes

1. New Testament scholar William E. Hull composed this commentary on John's Gospel, found in volume 9 of the Broadman Bible Commentary from the old and excellent Broadman Press (1970).

2. Hull, commentary on John 3, p. 240.

3. Found in the same paragraph as the previous quote on p. 240.

Jesus and Baptists and Jews—Oy Vey!

Some of my all-time favorite people are Jewish. The Marx Brothers. Mel Brooks. Even my Lord and Savior is a Jew.

And then there's our local rabbi (sort of), Seth Oppenheimer. He is not ordained yet, so he's always quick to interject a "student-rabbi" correction whenever I introduce him as Rabbi Seth.

The first time I heard Seth singing lines from Kinky Friedman's "They Ain't Makin' Jews Like Jesus Anymore,"[1] I knew we were going to be friends—and good friends we are. We get together regularly at the local tavern, along with the occasional priest and several friends,[2] to talk about faith and everything else under the sun. Sometimes he even shows up at the church where I pastor.[3]

I don't know if our friendship has helped make him a better Jew, but I do know it has helped me become a better Christian.

I've been reading the two-volume book series *Mount and Mountain*—conversations between two friends who are somewhat like Seth and me.[4] Two Tennessee clergymen, Rabbi Rami Shapiro and Reverend Michael Smith, examine together the Ten Commandments (volume 1) and the Sermon on the Mount (volume 2).

Rami and Mike bring into this dialogue their scholarship (each has a PhD and is involved in higher education), varying interpretations from within their respective traditions, their own opinions, and, of course, their trust and respect for each other. It is the latter that is most important, I think.

Both Mike and I come from the rich Baptist tradition of our Christian faith, specifically being Baptist in the Deep South. It is from this tradition that we learned to respect others, to listen to alternative and opposing viewpoints, and—above and beyond all doctrine and all professed beliefs—to seek to hold Jesus Christ (whom Baptists have historically proclaimed to be the ultimate revelation of God to humanity) as our fundamental center who guides our actions as his disciples. Jesus seemed pretty good at following the golden rule, and it only seems natural that if we claim his name, we should strive to treat others the way we would want others to treat us.

At the same time, within our Baptist heritage in the Deep South there arose a movement that focused less on the radically inclusive nature of Jesus and more on clearly defining and enforcing doctrinal statements, preferring not to serve others but to erect walls separating and protecting "Christians" from people with different life experiences and with alternative or opposing viewpoints. From that stream came the now infamous 1980 statement from Bailey Smith, then-president of the Southern Baptist Convention, "God Almighty does not hear the prayer of a Jew."[5]

Almost thirty years later, a fellow Baptist pastor asked to meet with me; he was concerned that I had been deceived regarding the status of Jews in the eyes of God. Judaism, the pastor stated, promoted the worship of a false god, a god that in no way even resembled the God of Jesus and God as revealed in the Christian Bible. That last statement still gets me; after all, the overwhelming majority of the Christian Bible is, ironically, Jewish.

Both the concerns of a ministerial colleague and the 1980 quote from an SBC president are examples of why books like the *Mount and Mountain* series are so important.

For understanding.

For humility.

For Christians seeking to know the God of Abraham, Moses, Jesus, and the Apostle Paul, and for those seeking to follow in the footsteps of Jesus (who himself worshiped in the Jewish temple).

Mike Smith and Rami Shapiro do not agree on everything. Nor do they water down their beliefs or their traditions. But they do listen to each other, and each is willing to acknowledge that God as revealed in the Bible is far bigger than any of our limited human understandings of God.

In examining the Ten Commandments and the Sermon on the Mount, Mike and Rami push, probe, and challenge each other. They discuss everything from poverty, wealth, "inerrancy," and interpretation to suffering, suicide, the nature of God, and what God requires of us.

Reading the *Mount and Mountain* books is an informative and enjoyable experience. They remind me that I am not alone in treasuring my friendship with a rabbi and in sensing his deep love for God that guides his interpretations and his daily actions. As a Christian, I am not threatened by Seth Oppenheimer, but rather encouraged and strengthened in my faith in God.

Mike Smith rightly points out that his and Rami's friendship may help them to hear some things that they'd rather not hear; I know that's true in my friendship with Seth. I agree with Mike when he writes, "Perhaps friendship should become the prerequisite to interfaith conversation."[6]

True friendship requires a lot of hard work, not to mention trust and respect. Sometimes it's easier to fall back on easy-to-spout doctrinal judgments rather than to invest in learning about and understanding others.

Or, if I may quote Rabbi Rami, "This is America, and here ignorance trumps scholarship almost every time . . . ."[7]

And to that I add, if I may quote my Jewish friends, "Oy vey!"

I can think of nothing better right now than to spend a couple of hours with my friend soaking in some Jewish wisdom. Just let me grab my Mel Brooks DVDs . . . .

Notes

1. If you're easily offended, do *not* do a web search for this song. If you're *not* easily offended, go for it! You'll be glad you did.

2. Yep—"A rabbi, a priest, and a preacher walk into a bar . . . ."

3. So this rabbi walks into a Baptist church . . . stop me if you've heard it . . . .

4. Both volumes of the *Mount and Mountain* series are available from Smyth & Helwys Publishing, just like the book you are holding now.

5. You'll just have to Google it—there's plenty available about it on the Internet. Lord, have mercy; Christ, have mercy . . . .

6. Says the preacher in *Mount and Mountain*, vol. 2 (on the Sermon on the Mount) 232.

7. Says the rabbi in *Mount and Mountain*, vol. 2 (on the Sermon on the Mount) 200.

Brother with a Semicolon

(Ode to Reverend Will D. Campbell)

In fall 2004, I took a seminary course on Thomas Merton. It was taught by Merton friend and scholar E. Glenn Hinson. Dr. Hinson knew of my near-obsession with all things Will Campbell, and he helped arrange a trip in which he and I would travel together to visit with Campbell at his home in Mt. Juliet, Tennessee. In addition to simply getting to hang out with Will Campbell, I planned to set up a recorder and let Campbell and Hinson swap their stories about and memories of Thomas Merton. I would then write a paper and submit it for a project grade for the course.

Less than two weeks before our trip, Will called me and said that he'd been thinking a lot about it, and his memories of and experiences with Merton were too personal, that he'd prefer not to talk about them. After all, Merton himself wrote a little about their friendship in his journals, and I could read about everything in there. Campbell really treasured his Merton memories and didn't want to talk much about them, so he canceled our meeting and asked me to give his greetings to Glenn Hinson. He did, however, invite me down simply to visit with him any time, which I of course did—once. We talked about everything, including his friendship with Waylon Jennings (one of my musical heroes). We didn't, however, talk much about Merton.

I never presumed to think of myself as a friend of Will's, but he was very gracious to me; we corresponded a few times over the years, and we'd talk on the phone from time to time—a couple of times he even called me! One of the greatest thrills of my life was when he agreed to consider writing a preface for my second book, *Psychic Pancakes & Communion Pizza*. With his permission, I sent him an advanced manuscript, but that ended up being about the time that he was not able to do much at all anymore, and soon he was in the hospital. Even though he didn't write the preface, I can still tell people that Will Campbell agreed to read my manuscript. Whether or not he actually read it, as far as I'm concerned, is moot.

During the time when Glenn Hinson and Will Campbell and I were planning our Thomas Merton summit, I had to have surgery to remove twelve inches of my colon (due to severe diverticulosis). Will told me over the phone that I had nothing to worry about; he'd had the same problem and had the same surgery done many years before. He then added, however, that his heart actually stopped at some point during the surgery, and he had to be resuscitated.

"You mean I was actually dead there on the operating table?" Will asked the surgeon during a follow-up meeting.

"Yep—for about three minutes you were dead."

To which Will replied, "Can I get you to sign an affidavit saying I was dead for three days? I've got a few people I'd like to show that to."

That was 100 percent pure Will Campbell.

When I was leaving Kentucky to pastor in Mississippi, Will told me about a recent experience of his with the University of Mississippi.[1] Ole Miss folks invited Will back down to Oxford;[2] they wanted to name him "Chaplain for Life."

Will said he hemmed and hawed and reminded them that the last time he was in Oxford, he was followed up to the state line by men in cars who pointed their guns at him, and when he crossed over into Tennessee, they threatened to kill him if he ever set foot back in Mississippi.

Therefore, said Will, he figured he'd pass on that chaplain-for-life thing. "Oh, but Reverend Campbell," they replied, "we've been reading all your stuff over these last many years about forgiveness and reconciliation and all that—and we figured you *meant* it." Will, recognizing that they had him on that one, grumbled and complained and cursed, then came down and "accepted their little piece of paper."

Much in my conversations with Will is really special to me, and I prefer not to talk about it. Since his passing, many have been and will continue to be writing about their memories of and experiences with Will Campbell—and rightfully so. I look forward to reading them. But

I now understand why Will chose to keep his Merton memories to himself.

Thank you, Will, for everything. Oh, and please give my greetings to Waylon.

Notes

1. I was coming to pastor University Baptist Church in Starkville, home of Ole Miss's archrival Mississippi State University.

2. Ole Miss had run him off while he served as campus minister there due to his insistence on living out racial equality. This was before James Meredith and the federal government successfully integrated the university.

Listening to the Dead

In fall of 1980, when I was twelve years old, I went with my dad into downtown New Orleans to his office on Magazine Street. Driving down Canal Street, the home of the beautiful and historic Saenger Theatre, I noticed something strange happening, and the Saenger Theatre was the epicenter of it all.

The Grateful Dead was set to play a few nights at the Saenger, which meant that a few days before the first show, Deadheads from everywhere converged upon New Orleans and set up camp along and all around Canal Street. Being a budding student of all things 1960s, this fascinated me to no end. Though I've never been an honest-to-goodness tie-dyed-in-the-wool Deadhead, it was about that time that I really became interested in the group. It was about that time, in my preteen years, that I began listening to the Dead.

Listening to the dead . . .

In perhaps one of the funniest Three Stooges short films, Shemp dies and then is sent back as a ghost to try to reform the cheating, lying, and face-slapping Moe and Larry—assuming, of course, that Moe and Larry will listen to the dead.

Charles Dickens brings Jacob Marley's ghost back to haunt Ebenezer Scrooge and to announce the coming of the Ghosts of Christmases past, present, and future. Why? To bring about a conversion of sorts, a reformation of Scrooge's greedy, merciless, and isolated self—assuming, of course, that Scrooge will listen to the dead.

Listening to the dead . . .

Jesus tells a story about a nameless rich man.[1] The rich man, who thoroughly enjoyed everything his money could buy, was blind to the needs of another right outside his window.

The rich man was deaf to the cries of a person in great need—crying at the end of the driveway every time the rich man drove by in his top-of-the-line luxury car. He never paid any attention to poor Lazarus reaching out for some assurance that his humanity mattered.

The only thing Lazarus ever got was a good view of the rich man's Deadhead sticker on the back of his Cadillac.[2]

But little did the rich man know that, even with buildings named in his honor at the universities and denominational offices and local church compounds, he was blocking out God. For God came to the rich man seeking compassion. God came to the rich man seeking mercy. God came to the rich man seeking mere crumbs from the table. God came to the rich man as one of the very "least of these," but the rich man never saw, never heard.

By building his barriers to keep the comfortable in and the uncomfortable out, he had also put God "out of sight" and therefore "out of mind."

When both die, though, it is Lazarus that is hanging out with Father Abraham, while the rich man is now suffering down in Hades. The last has been made first. The valley has been brought up, and the mountain has been made low.

In the spirit of Uncle Mortimer sending Shemp back from the dead, the rich man begs Father Abraham to send Lazarus back from the dead to warn and reform his brothers. But, as Jesus points out in the story, people have more than enough opportunities from those living around them to hear the Truth and follow the Way; people simply are not prone to listen to the dead.

People simply are not prone to listen to the dead.

Thousands and thousands of years of teachings and examples of compassion, mercy, community, sacrifice . . . and thousands and thousands of years of selfishness, greed, isolation, war.

If only we knew that in building our walls and putting up our fences and locking our doors and turning up our radios, we were not only securing ourselves from unpleasant sights, smells, and sounds around us but also securing ourselves from God.

And if we won't even listen to our Scriptures today . . .

And if we won't even heed the words of the prophets today . . .

Why, then, would we listen to the dead?

Listening to the dead . . .

The first of only two speeding tickets I have ever received in all my years of driving occurred early one morning on my way to work. I was driving along a wide-open four-lane highway with little traffic. A great song came on the radio, and as great songs are wont to do, it entranced me. My trance was broken when I noticed the police car right behind me. I got clocked doing a whopping 8 miles per hour over the speed limit.

The song? "Baba O'Reilly."

It is a great song, of course, but it's by the Who.

Had I been listening to the Dead, perhaps I never would have gotten into trouble.

If we would just listen to the dead . . .

But then again, so few of us will even listen to the living.

Notes

1. Read all about it here: Luke 16:19-31.

2. Thanks, Don Henley, for that terrific summation of the rise of the yuppies!

James's Amazing Grace Gumbo[1]

One of my first published columns declared Willie Nelson a saint. Willie appears a lot in my writings, and every so often someone politely reminds me that when he's not singing really great hymns and spirituals, Willie does a lot of other things that obviously disqualify him from sainthood. Therefore, as a minister of the gospel, I must be more discerning toward whom I point as an example of Christian virtue.

Thomas Merton wrote that "the stamp of grace is on the memory of yesterday."[2] Merton was writing about himself and his coming to accept and embrace, rather than be ashamed of and try to hide, his past. But that phrase—"the stamp of grace is on the memory of yesterday"—illuminates our willingness to judge a person less and less as more and more time passes since that person died. In about seventy-five years, people may very well remember the more godly things about Willie, but for now, well . . . I'm just avoiding the rush and getting an early start.

Merton's words are important as we consider these brief passages from the letter of James, especially since James is commonly understood as a "works-rather-than-grace" epistle. Such a generalization is not fair to James; in fact, in light of Merton's phrase, we may find that grace abounds throughout, despite the lack of attention it receives from a surface reading.

James quickly tosses some names out there as examples of faith in action. But when we take the time to consider all the baggage that goes with those names, we have to wonder why anyone would consider them to be "good examples." Let's take a look at James's use of Abraham, Rahab, and Elijah as edifying figures.

Abraham

> Was not our ancestor Abraham justified by works when he offered his son Isaac on the altar? You see that faith was active along with his works, and faith was brought to completion by the works. Thus the scripture was fulfilled that says, "Abraham believed God, and it was reckoned to him as righteousness," and he was called the friend of God. You see that a person is justified by works and not by faith alone. (James 2:21-24, NRSV)

Let's face it—Abraham was an old codger who at times seemed to wonder what kind of joke God was playing on him; that is, after he got up off the floor and dusted himself off where he had just fallen on his face laughing at God's joke about fathering a child at one hundred years of age with his old lady (in the literal sense of an old, and in this case barren, woman).

Who could blame Abe? After all, God said as much some years earlier, and Sarah, good wife that she was, decided that since she wasn't going to be able to do her part, she would volunteer her maid, Hagar, to be her surrogate; but then Sarah got mad and made everybody miserable, especially the pregnant Hagar, who fled. God, though, told Hagar to go back, which she did, reigniting the marital discord, which only worsened when Abe's son, Ishmael, was born. That's a lot of drama for a man in his mid-eighties.

At this point, the "father of many nations" has one son whom his wife resents even though it was her idea, until God blesses Sarah with a baby boy. It is sometimes said that every blessing is also a curse, and for Abe, while the new child now doubles his likelihood of fathering many nations, it also quadruples the domestic woe until, desperate for a moment of peace and quiet and in an attempt to please Sarah, he sends Hagar and Ishmael away for good.

Oh, and sometime after figuratively cutting himself off from one son, God tells him to do the same with the other, Isaac—albeit in a bit more literal manner. Given Sarah's demanding disposition when it comes to all things maternal, Abe decides it is best not to worry her about it. We know the ending of that story, of course, but one has to think Abraham, not Kristofferson, may be the one who first asked, "Why me, Lord?"

Rolling on the floor laughing at God rarely counts as good, faith-like behavior, but to keep going when it appears that you may be losing your mind does. Being willing to sacrifice Isaac and then still live with Sarah afterward, let alone himself, is just plain crazy. That, or it's the blending of faith and works together that marked Abraham as a friend of God. The latter is how James preferred to record it, with a stamp of grace.

Rahab

> Likewise, was not Rahab the prostitute also justified by works when she welcomed the messengers and sent them out by another road? For just as the body without the spirit is dead, so faith without works is also dead. (James 2:25-26)

Sing along, if you know the words: "There is a house in Jericho, they call the Rising Sun, and it's been the ruin of many a poor boy . . . ."[3]

Rahab could have run a thriving business in New Orleans, and no doubt many a Baptist minister would have tried to save her soul, until the visits cost some of them their marriages and their churches. We don't know much else about Rahab except that, being the kind of woman she was, she wasn't always keen on following the rule of law and therefore probably found it a bit thrilling to play a game of hide and seek with the king's men, thereby helping the Hebrew spies sent into Jericho by Joshua. We're not told exactly why the spies sent to Jericho ended up at Rahab's place (perhaps they were aspiring young Baptist preachers), but as it turns out, it was the madam who did the saving. And for that, James applies the stamp of grace upon the memory of Rahab and mentions her in passing as another example of righteousness through faith and works.

Elijah

> Therefore confess your sins to one another, and pray for one another,
> so that you may be healed. The prayer of the righteous is powerful
> and effective. Elijah was a human being like us, and he prayed
> fervently that it might not rain, and for three years and six months
> it did not rain on the earth. Then he prayed again, and the heaven
> gave rain and the earth yielded its harvest. (James 5:16-18, NRSV)

I sometimes imagine Elijah the prophet as a professional wrestler on
television—strutting, bragging, trash-talking, and challenging his arch-
nemesis not to just any old steel-caged match but to a non-sanctioned,
no-holds-barred, with-extra-obstacles-tossed-into-the-ring-to-make-it-
even-more-fun steel-caged match. A little while later, a new
arch-nemesis appears, the girlfriend of the previous arch-nemesis, and
she struts and brags and smashes chairs while stating what she's going
to do to Elijah . . . and Elijah cowers, hides, and cries like a baby.

A stickler for the law would question why anyone would point to
Elijah as an example of faith in action. When he was "up," he was
overdramatic, arrogant, and obnoxious. He had an antagonist edge that
kept him in conflict with the majority of folks most of the time. And
when he was "down" . . . well, that unstable emotional pendulum
swung hard and fast and wide, and there didn't appear to be much faith
at work when those mean woman blues drove Elijah to crawl inside a
hole and wait to die. Noting that Elijah was really not all that different
from any one of us, with all of our quirks and issues, James just throws
Elijah's name out there as an example of a righteous man praying.
Covering the width of Elijah's mood swings with grace requires a rather
large stamp.

A Taste of Grace

With clear directives on how to pray, what one should and shouldn't say
about the future, how to anoint with oil one who needs healing, and a
strong emphasis on social action toward the poor, hungry, and outcast,
James's letter can come across as perhaps the most legalistic book in the
New Testament. Yet, when we take the time to savor the flavor—like a

Cajun making gumbo, James stirs in a heaping amount of Abraham, a good sprinkling of Elijah, and just a pinch of Rahab (only a pinch; she's very spicy)—we'll taste the richness of grace in which everything else rests.

As Merton said, "the stamp of grace is on the memory of yesterday," and this is certainly true with the letter of James. A reckless reading sees legalism, but a hearty bite tastes grace through and through.

Now, let's all stand and sing as St. Willie leads us in a rousing rendition of "Amazing Grace."

Notes

1. "James's Amazing Grace Gumbo" originally appeared in *The Letter of James*, Christian Reflection: A Series in Faith and Ethics 42 (Waco TX: Center for Christian Ethics at Baylor University, 2012) 79–82. It is reprinted by permission of the publisher.

2. Thomas Merton wrote this in his book *The Sign of Jonas* (San Diego: Harcourt, Inc., 1981) 32. As a side note, had Merton not died in 1968, I'm convinced that he would have come to absolutely love Willie Nelson.

3. "House of the Rising Sun" is a traditional folk song most widely associated with the blues-rock arrangement that gave the Animals a number-one hit single. Granted, some interpret this song to be about gambling and drinking (and it is), but generally folks think of it primarily as a song about Rahab's line of work.

Part 2

Conversations & Such

Nig*@# Please!

(Talking the "N-word" with Oteil Burbridge)

Oteil Burbridge is an internationally renowned bass-guitar funkmeister who plays just about anywhere with just about anybody when he's not busy touring as the bassist with the Allman Brothers Band. We recently sat down to talk[1] about Huck Finn, the "N-word," and other such things.

BERT: Hey, Oteil—interested in talking about the "N-word" . . . you and me? A honky and a Negro?[2]

OTEIL: Nigga, please! It's one of my biggest causes! "Nigger" is simultaneously one of my favorite, and least favorite, words. *Blazing Saddles* is my favorite movie, so I'm always harping on this. I love how Mel Brooks dealt with it. That movie couldn't be made today.

BERT: The newly sanitized rewriting of Mark Twain's *Huckleberry Finn* bothers me. Why are we afraid to allow it [the word "nigger"] to be said in its historical context? I believe in letting the word exist lest we forget the intention behind it. I think it's sort of like everyone in the Harry Potter stories refusing to say the name "Voldemort."

OTEIL: This situation is *exactly* like "He-Who-Must-Not-Be-Named." I think until blacks give up using the word, then no one else should have to.

BERT: Does it offend you to hear white people say "nigger"? I'll be honest—I feel very uncomfortable saying it to you right now.

OTEIL: One of my white friends is as big of a *Blazing Saddles*/Richard Pryor/Dave Chappelle fan as I am. We realized how silly this word's power was when he and his friends were afraid to quote parts of Pryor's routines for fear of offending me. I was stupefied because I realized what an awkward position we let a mere word put us in. It also taught me that the tongue is in fact mightier than the sword. If a white (or black) person doesn't mean it in a hurtful way, I don't take it that way. If my white friend is merely quoting our favorite part of a Richard Pryor routine, then why would it offend me?

BERT: Yeah, but eventually, Pryor made a public renunciation of "nigger" and quit using it. It was after a trip he took to Africa.

OTEIL: I remember when that happened to Richard. It was pretty profound for him, I think, because he had never been in a country where black people ran everything. In his mind, black people were always the underdog. But he is wrong when he says that the word "nigger" only means one thing. He forgets that Nigeria and the Niger River have something to do with it, too. While Richard may later have repudiated that word, he also popularized its use in the context of stand-up comedy. I think that scared him later—and with good reason. Most of the other black comics use it because it gives them a sense of rebellion. Dave Chappelle is the only one I've seen so far that actually uses our preoccupation with, and feelings toward, the word more than the word itself. Richard made a career out of more than just that word, though. His characters were what really captured people. But characters like Mudbone said "nigger" a lot. Richard was being funny and used street language. That's how everyone talked in the ghetto (or in the country like with Mudbone), and he just reflected that. I'm really glad Richard co-wrote *Blazing Saddles* with Mel Brooks before he "converted."

BERT: Do you use the "N-word"?

OTEIL: For my specific white friend and me, it actually is now the highest compliment that we could pay somebody. In our world only niggas . . .

BERT: "Niggas"?

OTEIL: Make sure you pronounce it "nigga," please. It makes all the difference! The -er on the end really can get you killed!

BERT: Thanks for the heads up . . .

OTEIL: Anyway, in our world only niggas can accomplish certain things (whether they be white or black). Dick Cheney could never funk like James Brown and Sly Stone, or make you cry like Mahalia or Aretha, or make you laugh with characters like Richard Pryor or Dave Chappelle. This also implies (in our reversed world) that Jesus is the HNIC and Satan is Whitey.

BERT: Um . . . HNIC?

OTEIL: Head Nigga In Charge.

BERT: Ahhh . . .

OTEIL: Conversely, "Whitey" is a state of mind and not limited to race. Any oppressor is "Whitey." When we say "kill Whitey" we don't mean a specific race. Mobutu is Whitey, too.

BERT: I'm still stunned by your description of Jesus as the HNIC . . .

OTEIL: I love Tony Campolo's story about the pastor who preached that Jesus was a nigger because he purposely came to earth to be a slave, to be despised, to be wronged, etc. . . . Jesus said that "the last would be first." So who would have been first to inherit the kingdom of God throughout most of this country's history?

BERT: Wow—that's powerful! The Gospel according to Oteil . . .

OTEIL: I want to clarify that when I say that "'nigger' is simultaneously my favorite and least favorite word," I am referring to what is essentially two different words, reflected by their different spellings. And I want to clarify that the reason it would even be my favorite word at all is because it focuses like a laser on so much that we need to get past in this country. Racism is the defining issue of my parents' life and many others' as well. It's hard for younger non-black people to understand how much of an impact it has had. While I think we need to get past it and realize that *all* people are "fallen" and will divide and segregate over any tribal difference (race, religion, ideology, nation, language . . .), we also can't pretend racism never happened/happens in this specific way against blacks in this country. To take this word's power away, it will require us to not be in denial of it through banning use of the word. Some blacks will not give up using it anytime soon anyway. I probably won't either. Making white people who are true fans of Richard Pryor or Dave Chappelle feel guilty about repeating some of their funniest lines is also ridiculous. Of course, a lot of blacks' attitudes towards each other concerning color and hair are pretty ridiculous and surprising. I say we *all* cut the crap and just call a spade a spade. Sorry, I just couldn't resist . . .

BERT: Care to explain that?

OTEIL: Have you seen the movie *Good Hair* by Chris Rock? It's a friggin' mind blower. Many in the black community are just as self-hating, prejudiced, and homophobic as anyone else. A black friend told me that a lady at a bar once told him that he was very nice and that she really liked him a lot, but that she could never really be with him because he wasn't quite dark enough. Strange criteria.

BERT: Thanks for your time, Oteil. Got any last words?

OTEIL: Yeah—Kill Whitey! *(laughing)*

Notes

1. "Sat down to talk," as used here means "sat down with our computers and exchanged several e-mails."

2. Just to be clear—I'm the honky.

Faith, Self-Discovery, and Christian Music

(An Interview with Ex-Altar Boy Ric Alba)

Ric Alba is a legend to fans of 1980s alternative/punk/new-wave Christian rock. He played bass on Undercover's eponymous debut album and then went on to play with the Altar Boys. He released one solo album before "coming out of the closet" and disappearing from the Christian music scene. As you are about to find out, Ric's musical journey is almost as eclectic as his personal journey—a search filled with certainty, denial, confusion, spiritual manipulation, emotional abuse, acceptance, and hope and love.

Today, Ric and his partner own an interior design firm in California. Ric still plays music, most notably recording a new Dead Artist Syndrome (DAS) album with a fellow legend of the alternative Christian music genre, Brian Healy.

BERT: Back in the '80s, folks sometimes promoted Christian artists as "the Christian alternative" to secular artists. As in, "if you're a Christian and you like this secular artist, then you should be listening to this Christian artist." Were you thinking about that while you were a part of the CCM scene?

RIC: I think nearly all bands are in one way or another doing what somebody else started, while sometimes pointing fingers and calling others derivative. But it's no crime. Just as in the secular world, bands take after other bands that inspired them, and so did we. We played the way we felt inspired to play. In the evangelical world, though, it was expected that the bands had evangelical reasons for whatever we did. If a band reminded one of say, The Clash, then it was presumed that band's purpose was to evangelize fans of The Clash. Navigating our way through the evangelical industry, eventually I realized that it got the job done to go ahead and let it be painted like that's what we were doing if that's how people needed to paint it. They had their reasons, I'm sure, and I have no reason to say their hearts weren't pure. But really, we were all just playing the way we enjoyed playing, inspired by and building on the work of those who were already playing that way. We said that a lot, but some folks still kept wanting to paint it as a calculated evangelical strategy. Oh well, okay . . . my, what brilliant evangelical strategists we all were!

BERT: You're a Christian. And, you're gay.

RIC: I have to say right off that because of my current approach to faith, it's best that I don't claim the name "Christian" for myself. The controversy of who is qualified for that name distracts from more important things, so I'll just be who I am, say what I feel, and let people call me what they want, if anything. I understand that for many people, it hurts to hear me say that because so many of my favorite people throughout my life have been those I know from my years as an evangelical. Those relationships are still valuable to me, and I'm in a place of transition, from being somewhat in opposition to a life of faith, toward embracing one for myself. Most of the Christians I interact with today regard me as one of their own, and I cherish that. The language of my thoughts on God today comes from all that I learned, sought, and experienced when I was a Christian. In that sense, there's a kinship I feel with Christians that will more likely grow from here than weaken.

I stopped identifying as a Christian after being excommunicated by the Anaheim Vineyard in 1991. At the time, I couldn't reconcile being gay with being a Christian. I was in a process of trying to do that when I got a call from my church telling me to come to their offices and explain myself in regard to sexuality. They told me that if I failed to show, they'd pray to release me to Satan so he could kill me before I "fell too far into my sin." That right there was my clue that things there had gotten too wacko for me to remain there without going completely insane. My refusal to obey at that moment was a kind of self-rescue. I didn't seem to have anywhere else to go, though, in 1991, so I went nowhere in terms of a faith community.

BERT: Tell me about your struggles between being Christian and being gay. When did you sense you were gay?

RIC: My earliest crushes, maybe around age seven or so, were on other boys my age, and I knew right then that that might be out of the ordinary, but I didn't panic over it. It wasn't until years later when the word "fag" started getting thrown at me on the schoolyard that I realized that liking other guys was such a big taboo. I actually had to ask a classmate what the word meant, and when he told me I thought, "What's the big deal?" Thankfully I had enough friends outside of school who liked me enough for my musical abilities to overlook the things that my schoolmates bullied me for. I lived comfortably in their company, playing in cover bands throughout high school until the last of those bands broke up.

Then in 12th grade I became a born-again Christian, and for the first couple years I basked in the belief that nothing about my past life mattered, because I was a "new creature." It saved me from the work of having to deal with anything at all about myself, as long as I did all the things I was told to do as a Christian. It was like not even having to acknowledge my own existence. The teaching was to "die to self." It totally stunted my growth. Denying myself a gay love life wasn't too hard for me back then. I was a very late bloomer when it came to sex drive. I simply lived celibate, and was grateful for a community that made it easy to do that, with its prohibitions on fornication.

But eventually adulthood caught up with me, and so did sexuality. In 1980 I went for counseling at Vineyard about it. Their response was to "pray the gay away." I prayed, and they said to get on with my life and forget the whole thing, as an act of faith in my healing. I became very close friends with a girl I met there, and we got married. Problem solved, so I thought. But no, by the mid-1980s it was clear to me that I was more "same-sex attracted" than ever, but I still didn't act on it.

BERT: How did you respond? Denial? Prayer? Reparative therapy? You were in the Altar Boys at the time, weren't you?

RIC: HUGE denial. I wouldn't even dare think the words, "I'm gay." I developed a unique way of thinking about it. I developed this theory that there was no such thing as gayness, and that we were all the victims of some kind of societal effect that was robbing everyone of the love they deserved. I theorized that everyone felt a coldness and was seeking warmth in various, destructive ways. In my thinking, same-sex attraction was the result of being intuitive enough to notice that something (I had no theory on what, exactly) was missing in all of society, including Christian society. I prayed and prayed for Jesus to finally come in person and fill in the blanks that he'd left behind when he was last seen in person 2,000 years before. That was how I framed everything.

That was my only hope, thinking that Christianity as it was, was incomplete, that there was supposed to be something more, a key of some kind that Jesus would bring someday. In my thinking, openly gay people had given up and settled for less. I thought of gay sexual activity as "The fires of hell—which do give warmth, but dude, it's hell."

The idea of a happy gay life well-lived was foreign to me, and my religion prohibited me from even entertaining the idea that a gay life could be a happy one. It was over the course of those years that the songs for *Holes in the Floor of Heaven*[1] developed. In public, church, and before my own eyes, I didn't dare let myself be "me." The imagery of *Holes* is loaded with the sounds of someone real, pleading for a way to be unlocked from deep within someone who was not so real, and who was deathly afraid of the person inside.

It got to be totally obvious that the right thing to do was to tell my wife all about what I was going through. The next step after that was to go back to Vineyard and ask for counseling. They recommended a facility (which turned out to be an inpatient clinic) that offered an early form of reparative therapy on a 12-step model. During that time, our hopes for a marriage and family started to fade. I did one more tour with Altar Boys, then left the band and started college in hopes of saving my marriage. No—the therapy had absolutely no affect on my sexual orientation. My wife and I separated right about the time I started recording *Holes*. Then . . . the excommunication.

BERT: You left the Altar Boys and the Christian music subculture in which you were living in order to be openly gay. How did folks respond?

RIC: Oh, when I left the Altar Boys in late 1990, I had no intention of living a gay life of any kind. I left in order to go to school full-time while pursuing a path to putting out *Holes in the Floor of Heaven*, once it was clear that our label wouldn't do it. I never made my personal struggles clear within the Altar Boys' circle.

With very few exceptions, I didn't give them a chance to [respond]. It wasn't until 1992, some time after having been excommunicated, I started living a gay love life and disappeared from Christendom so profoundly it was like faking my own death. During the Altar Boys, I had formed so many friendships with fans, who I feared, perhaps wrongly, were too young and impressionable to have to deal with this change in me, so I went quietly into the night. Touring as a Christian musician to support *Holes in the Floor of Heaven* was out of the question because that would mean living in a closet. By that time, I was involved in helping to alleviate the AIDS crisis, which had been caused in great part by society forcing gay people into closets.

BERT: How did you come to accept your sexuality within your faith?

RIC: For some years after my excommunication, I had no faith in anything "unseen" except the conviction that if God exists, He is a lover of truth, including the truth that the belief system I had lived in for so long had serious problems that made it impossible for me to stay in it. I rested peacefully, knowing that if God existed He would find me, and that whatever the two of us work out will be entirely different from my previous life of faith.

BERT: Tell me a little about your current approach to faith.

RIC: I have to start by offering that I could be wrong about everything I say about who or what lies beyond the senses. It's okay, though, because I don't think that having correct beliefs is what matters to the person or persons we seek as the objects of our faith. What is important, what I feel responsible for, is building within myself a good heart and mind.

Part of that process for me these days is being aware of the possibility that more "exists" than what can yet be detected by our current senses and instruments. So, I don't say conclusively that there are no such things as unseen beings. I like the idea that they are around. But I do say that whatever is actually "out there," their nature and intention is anyone's guess, so while we're all guessing, and using our imaginations, I find it both challenging and comforting to envision things that help me to live an authentic life, to love and be loved, to be more kind, patient, helpful, truthful, and all those good things we aspire to be while on the Earth.

Because of my experiences as a "born-again Christian," I developed a way of thinking that I still have. It was a part of my Christianity, and now it's an indelible part of me. What I'm talking about is that I still live under the impression that my comings and goings are being played out in front of an unseen audience, which I'm still unapologetically accustomed to calling, "The Kingdom of God." In my impression, it's an audience that patiently watches as I go through life and learn my lessons. Partly out of habit, and partly out of desire, the mental image I keep, which represents that "unseen audience," is Jesus. Of course that fact doesn't obligate myself or anyone to accept the whole package of any named religion. It's just that I was raised to be, and then chose to be, a Christian; so when I picture unseen beings from unseen realms who look on our world with an interest in our well-being, that's the image I have, and I'm good with that.

I don't apologize to my "believing" side for the absence of orthodoxy, and I don't apologize to my skeptical side for maintaining that tiny aspect of faith. Both of those sides of me have been learning to accept one another.

So even though I confidently agree with nearly every atheist on record, I think that in my exploration into faith I've done a good thing (harmless, too) by letting some of my past impressions about God remain as a part of my current reality. It goes along with accepting who I am as a person. Christian imagery, some of its moral philosophy, and a little bit of its theology have become an intractable part of this person I am, right along with other intractable parts that I learned to accept. It might sound like a mess trying to put it to words, but it's my truth as best I can share it without using music.

BERT: Let's get back to the music. Who were your biggest musical influences growing up?

RIC: Schroeder, from the Charlie Brown gang, gave me my first inspiration when I was around five. He was a little boy like me, but he was playing Beethoven's *Moonlight Sonata*, and I just assumed it's natural for little boys to be able to do that. I remember reaching up to my grandma's piano to feel out which keys made the song's opening three-note pattern, and found them. My dad ran out and got a piano, and I've been gradually figuring out that piece by ear ever since. I'm almost to the end, and I think I'll leave it where it is. Ludwig's ending drags out too long anyway. He'll thank me, and I'll accept the grade "F" I'll get from music teachers.

After that, the only music that existed for me until Led Zeppelin was The Beatles. I learned a lot of Paul's parts, then onto John Paul Jones, and would you believe, Gene Simmons, who was always underrated as a bassist. I still play those slapped parts from "Detroit Rock City" warming up the bass.

BERT: Today, what would you list as your favorite Altar Boys songs, and why?

RIC: The song "Against the Grain" is a champion among the songs Mike (Stand) and I co-authored, because it represents a sharp turning point. We'd sung so much up to that point about what was wrong with the world, but I wasn't really in the world that much. The church was my world, and yet it was still one that had all kinds of things wrong with it. "Against the Grain" was to me our first steps toward addressing that fact head-on, beginning with the question, "What do we mean by 'Christianity?'" "The Human Sound" is another along those lines. "Kids are On the Run" is simply a great song.

BERT: Are you working on anything new right now?

RIC: I've been working with Brian Healy on a new DAS project with Ojo Taylor, Gym Nicholson, Riki Michele, Marc Plainguet, John Picarri at the console, and a few TBA's. It's been steadily expanding as ideas keep coming.

Note

1. This is the title of Ric's 1991 solo album.

From Christian Punk to Agnostic Prof

(An Interview with Ojo Taylor)

In summer 1984, a friend gave me a tape with Undercover's self-titled debut on side one and their second album, *God Rules*, on the other. I was hooked immediately.

As I finished high school and entered college, my personal faith began to deepen and to make room for questions, doubts, and grace in the world. Interestingly, the guys in Undercover were maturing and also leaving behind the simplicity of their early lyrics. Today, I listen to those early Undercover albums with fondness and joy, and though I no longer believe in their simplistic and legalist-easy-answers lyrics, I am thankful that those albums came along in my life when they did.

A few years ago I connected via Facebook with Undercover leader Joey "Ojo" Taylor (who in the mid-80s, when I was in high school, was one of my heroes). Today, Ojo is a professor at James Madison University (and in the summers, at Cal State, Fullerton). He teaches classes like History of Rock, Songwriting, Artist Management, Legal Aspects of the Music Industry, and Music Marketing.

Neither Ojo nor I are the same as we were almost thirty years ago (thankfully!). While I still consider myself a Christian, Ojo, on the other hand, is an agnostic.

A few months ago, Ojo agreed to an email interview: I'd email him with questions and he'd reply. Here are the highlights of our email exchanges in which Ojo addresses musical influences, Undercover, and his own spiritual journey.

BERT: Who were some of your biggest musical influences growing up?

OJO: The only records I remember as a kid in the house were *Sing Along with Mitch*, the Jackie Gleason Orchestra, a record of ragtime piano songs, and a few others, but I listened to them all. I remember when my father bought Herb Alpert's record with the chick covered in whipped cream . . . I liked the record and, like many other young boys, liked the record cover too.

My mother's brother bought the first Beatles record when it came out and left it over at our house once. I was probably seven years old. That was it for me. Most of the rest of the decade was all about the Beatles. That's not a bad way to go, I suppose.

Then towards the end of the 1960s it was CSNY, Led Zeppelin, and most of the other popular records high school-aged boys liked. I won the first Jimi Hendrix album in a dance contest and that changed my life . . . . Although neither of my parents were big music consumers, they did love music and made sure I had piano lessons all the way through high school.

It was not till high school that I began buying records in earnest . . . James Gang; Santana; more Beatles; Black Sabbath; Deep Purple; Jethro Tull; Yes; Pink Floyd . . . . Pretty much the run-of-the-mill popular stuff, great as all that stuff may be. By the end of high school, I had a lot of records but had not even heard a note by Muddy Waters.

BERT: Prior to forming Undercover, were you in any other bands? Were they distinctively "evangelical/Christian" lyrically?

OJO: I didn't start playing in bands until I was eighteen and had just graduated from high school. I was invited to play in Gym Nicholson's band (the guitarist in Undercover) because he had heard that I played piano. Having taken piano lessons is nothing like playing in a band, though, and there was a learning curve. We began playing covers, high school dances, backyard parties, and stuff like that. We were not very good, but we were paying our dues. We went through a few iterations with different names and members, but Gym and I were always the constants. We became evangelical Christians a couple years later in

1976 and almost immediately began writing our own songs for the first time, and those with religious lyrics. The rest, as they say, is history.

BERT: Anyone who has kept up with you knows that you no longer adhere to Christianity or any religion for that matter. Do you consider yourself an atheist? Agnostic?

OJO: I try to dodge the labels because they are so arbitrary and misunderstood. I have no idea what I am. Or rather I am both or either of those things at one time or another. I don't want to get into technical definitions and stuff, and life isn't that way for me anyway. I know very few if any thoughtful atheists who insist that they know beyond any doubt that there is no god. Most atheists I know are also agnostic that way. Even Richard Dawkins says the same thing. We don't know for sure. But neither do we know with 100% certainty whether or not there are teapots between the Earth and sun, as Bertrand Russell used to say. We can probably safely say there are none, but we cannot prove that there are not. So it is with that distinction between atheism and agnosticism in some minds. We too often get stuck in the semantics.

Stephen Roberts summed it up (although there is some legitimate critique of the language he uses) when he said, "I contend that we are both atheists. I just believe in one fewer god than you do. When you understand why you dismiss all the other possible gods, you will understand why I dismiss yours." It is true, though, that we are all unbelievers with respect to all gods but our own if we assume that they are different gods rather than different versions of one God. The fact that I take it "one god further" in my inability to believe the Orthodox or evangelical Christian version of things is a big deal to many Christians. But let me put myself in some perspective if I may.

There was not a single moment when I woke up and "decided" I was now going to be an unbeliever. My faith was dismissed little by little over a number of years until at one point I realized there was just nothing left. I've documented some of those erosions on my blog[1] and in other places. In the end, I am probably an atheist in that I don't believe in a specific supernatural god nor do I have a coherent model for what that might look like nor a reason to embrace belief in one. It would be great if there was an all-loving God who would welcome us with life eternal at the end of our lives, but that wishful thinking is not enough to get me there. I am agnostic in that I don't know. There just might be a god out there! It's fluid, I am open, and I find no compelling reason to join myself to one label or the other. I'll leave that for others.

It was probably 2008 that I realized I could no longer call myself a Christian. The funny thing was that I felt no different inside, but just had that realization that I no longer could believe what I was being asked to believe. I still had some questions about things like the resurrection of Jesus and stuff like that, but I read and read and studied as much as I could. In the end, it was more a shift in the way I chose to evaluate claims than in choosing not to be a Christian anymore and to start living in some other way. I still was the same person, still committed to love, my family, to doing good, to making a positive impact in my world with the time I have. I just could not force myself to believe many of the objective claims that Christianity makes, and . . . once the doctrines are gone, then what's left? It is only love that is left for me. Some will say that's what Jesus was all about, but Jesus was about lots of other things too if we are to believe what is said about him in the Scriptures.

I am interested in faith. I am interested in it because it is a human phenomenon that has global consequences. We may not survive this century, and religion and its various worldviews will have a lot to do with that. I am interested in knowing more about it because I feel like I gave so much of my own life and time to it. How did that happen? Why? How does it work? What are the mechanisms? I am interested in it because I am interested in the universe and all that is real within it, visible or not visible, but real in any case.

I am not interested, however, in living a life of faith where I define what's real only by what some ancient text, tradition, or religious authority says. What I believe must now be earned, and I will put that bar for evidence as high as the seriousness of the claim and in direct proportion to the likelihood that those claims are true or not. Thomas Huxley said it better: "Trust a witness in all matters in which neither his self-interest, his passions, his prejudices, nor the love of the marvelous is strongly concerned. When they are involved, require corroborative evidence in exact proportion to the contravention of probability by the thing testified." Why should this be a controversial proposition to the religious? I believe it is only because it throws down the gauntlet, and for so many it calls into question the veracity of what they believe regarding objective claims about our universe in time-space. And then what, after the evidentiary house of cards falls?

BERT: During your journey . . . how were your Undercover bandmates reacting? The band as a whole certainly matured toward the end when compared to the catchy simplicity of the first two albums.

OJO: Well, yes, it's been a journey for all of us, and we did kind of "grow up in public" as has been said of us before. A few punches in the gut in the course of one's life will have a tendency to do that, to grow you up pretty quickly. I would say that the fundamentalism of our earliest days just didn't last that long, maybe the first three records, but by the third it was already becoming obvious to us all under the surface that we were going to be asking some questions rather than simply spitting out answers.

Over the years, we've all ended up in different places. It's pretty clear to me, and I don't even think about this that much, that our relationships with each other are not based on the band or on what we believe or not. It is very much like family. Our acceptance and affection for each other just "is." Having said that, I think my dismissal of faith has had an impact.

My skepticism has had the biggest impact probably on our two singers, Bill Walden and Sim Wilson. Bill is a pastor in Napa, California, and Sim is a pastor's son and is very active in his church in Cleveland, Tennessee, so I suppose that stands to reason. It has not negatively impacted anything in practice, as far as I can tell, but I think it does cause Sim some grief at least. To the others it has simply not been much of an issue at all.

BERT: What kind of "reception" have you received from other "Christian" musicians with whom you may have toured, played with, etc.? Have you lost any "friends"?

OJO: True friends are true friends, so anyone I've lost I have to think was lost before they were lost. I'll say this, and I hope it doesn't get me in too much trouble—there are a good many artists at various stages of doubt in their lives. Some are open about it, some are not. Some cannot be open because their livelihoods are connected to their religion. That's an awful place to be, but I guess it's inevitable and is probably the same for pastors. Where does a pastor with a family go once he or she has lost belief? For some artists it's simply a private matter and they don't feel compelled to talk about it openly.

I have had all kinds of comments, from the very nasty (although those are mostly from disgruntled fans) to threats to follow me around virtually and oppose things I say (this from a member of another band who I did not know well, but who had looked up to us), but most frequently, they express a sense of sadness and disappointment. I find that a very strange response indeed, and it's hard for me not to interpret it as a projection of a response to their own doubt onto me that somehow threatens their own faith. Some have encouraged me, and that mostly from other artists who also doubt at one level or another. But really, isn't every bit of growth we experience as human beings a result of doubt and skepticism? We leave things behind because we find they don't fit anymore, and often it's painful. Why should doctrinal tenets or objective claims made by religions be any different?

I have been having some really great dialogue with Michael Pritzl of The Violet Burning, a lifelong and very dear friend who has been completely accepting and respectfully curious. We learn from each other, and he has had his own journey from Catholicism to Evangelicalism and then to Anglicanism (I hope I am representing him correctly).

It's difficult to generalize. I know lots of people and have many friends. I'm very lucky that way. Some simply don't talk about it, I'm sure some are worried for the fate of my eternal soul (I've been told that too), some encourage me, some are Universalist so it doesn't matter what anyone believes or doesn't believe, some are too busy working out their own thing to worry about mine. I've heard it all. The bottom line though is that, for the most part, my dearest and closest friends are not going to throw our friendship away over something like doubt.

BERT: Were you (or are you) ever embarrassed by the '70s and '80s evangelical stage of your journey? Do your students research Undercover and ask you about "Talk to God" or "Jesus Girl" or "Slaughter of the Innocents"?

OJO: At one level, I can look back on all that and simply chalk it up to youth. That's where things were back then, and it would be a mistake to look at those songs outside the context of where the church was culturally and what they were able to accept and stomach at that time. The lyrics had to be overt, and the simpler, the better. By the time (our fourth album) *Branded* came around, I didn't care about that anymore. I needed to make the statement that album made. Today, everything in Christian music has pretty much been worked out. Christian bands can have careers outside of the Christian music industry, can have infidels as co-members, and can sing about whatever they want. In 1980 it wasn't that way.

I do not mean to rationalize or explain away those early days, though. Those songs and lyrics did represent where we were at that time, and what Christian life for young people was like in Orange County, California, and it does look awfully immature and shallow. In some ways that was really good for young people who attended church. They were able to break free of artificial cultural fetters within a lyrical framework of pretty conservative cheerleading that made things more acceptable for church leaders. That was a consequence, but the bottom line is that we did write those lyrics.

My students do look me up. It's impossible to hide. The song they most often want to hear is "God Rules," and I rarely indulge them, but then I don't need to really. It's all out there. They got a particular kick out of the version of "God Rules" set to *Family Guy* footage. I still don't know where that came from, but it's out there.

BERT: Occasionally you still get together with the other guys to play an Undercover show. . . . How do you feel about singing those songs today? Are there any from your Undercover catalog that you simply will not do? Why or why not?

OJO: I really think those days are winding down . . . . It's not the songs themselves; it's the politics and sociology around it. Yes, there are early lyrics I wrote and that we wrote and performed for years that I cringe to think about. "Slaughter of the Innocents" should be fully retracted and erased from the face of the earth. In classical music, the composer can recall a piece and that's the end of it; it's gone from the repertoire. Not so in popular music. There are some songs I simply will not play anymore because I think the lyrics are harmful, discriminatory, or just plain silly. There are others I won't play because they are not musically consistent with anything we've done lately, and there are some we won't play because they have little value beyond nostalgia and I'm not really into that.

On the other hand, there are some songs I enjoy playing because I like the music even though lyrically it may not be consistent with what I believe. They are not harmful, and the songs are often meaningful to people. There are some songs we play that we play because we love the music and the lyrics. "Build a Castle" and "So Wonderful" would be good examples of that last kind, and there are others. Some songs, like "Way of the Rose," are renderings of biblical events with no underlying message or doctrinal proposition. I'm okay with those, too. There are also times where another band member might feel strongly about playing or not playing a song. It's not all about me, and I am happy to support them too. It's a case-by-case thing. I think we're all on the same page roughly, though. There are some songs we simply will not play. The older the song, the more likely it is we've left it behind, although that is not always true.

Note

1. Visit Ojo at http://ojotaylor.wordpress.com/.

The "Lost" *Wittenburg Door* Interview with Baptist Heretic/Legend Dr. E. Glenn Hinson

In late summer/early fall 2007, I interviewed Dr. E. Glenn Hinson for the religious satire magazine The Wittenburg Door. *The contract was signed and the article sold; it was to appear in a spring 2008 edition. I never got paid as promised. But, to be fair, the interview was never published as promised. The legendary* The Wittenburg Door *just sort of disappeared into the night and has not been heard from since. Portions of this interview were released elsewhere online; but here, as it was to have been originally published, is my full interview with Dr. Hinson for* The Door. *As it was composed fall 2007 for a spring 2008 issue, Benedict was the "new" Pope, and George W. was in his second presidential term. Now then, imagine you've just received your brand new spring 2008 issue of* The Wittenburg Door.

Dr. E. Glenn Hinson. World-renowned church historian. Respected and sought-after leader in Christian Spirituality. And everyone's favorite living Baptist heretic.

When the opportunity arose to meet with Dr. Hinson at one of Louisville, Kentucky's finer pizza establishments, we jumped at the chance. Of course, if Albert Mohler offered to buy us pizza, we'd jump at the chance, too. (Call us when you're willing to talk, Al.)

But to sit down with one of the legends of Southern Baptist academic life—back when Southern Baptists had an academic life—and discuss everything from his former seminary (the Southern Baptist Theological Seminary in Louisville) to the President of the USA, and everything from the Pope to flatulence (yeah—it comes up) . . . c'mon! This gentle and unassuming 76-year-old man was personal friends with everyone's favorite Trappist monk, Thomas Merton. He has written what seems like hundreds of books (if you expect specifics, shouldn't you be reading something else?), including such classics as *Jesus Christ, The Integrity of the Church*, and everyone's favorite answer to "why pray?"—*A Serious Call to a Contemplative Lifestyle.*

And, during the years when he was actually *allowed* to teach Church History and Christian Spirituality at Southern Seminary, he was under constant attack for his heresies. Since that meant he didn't toe the Southern Baptist line, we knew we'd like this guy. We think you will, too. If not, you truly may be reading the wrong magazine (but keep subscribing; it pays our bills!).

DOOR: Tell us about teaching at Southern Seminary.

GLENN: I taught church history, and I tried to help the students to embrace church history as the history of us all. At that time, Southern offered freedom to do things like I did in 1960—taking my first class to the Abbey of Gethsemani. That was Providential in my view.

DOOR: Did you take them to meet Thomas Merton?

GLENN: I didn't really know about Thomas Merton. I took the students to expose them to the Middle Ages. I thought they'd learn more about the Middle Ages by going to a monastery than they would talking about it. Merton was our host. Immediately after we were there, he wrote to me, "Glenn, I'm coming to Louisville. I'd like to stop in and see you." I got our faculty together, and we spent two hours with Merton. That was great because it meant that many of those that were very suspicious of my taking students to Gethsemani got to know him.

DOOR: How long were you a Southern Seminary professor?

GLENN: My formal tenure on SBTS faculty was from 1962–1992, but I did teach three years before that—a full load.

DOOR: When did you become a favorite target of the fundamentalists?

GLENN: I became a target when I responded to Bailey Smith's comment in 1980, "God Almighty does not hear the prayer of a Jew." I was really a "fair-haired boy" before that.

DOOR: Your response was . . . ?

GLENN: I made five points in response to Bailey Smith: (1) Jesus was a Jew—you may have disenfranchised Jesus' prayers; (2) You disenfranchised everybody from Abraham to Jesus; (3) The Bible teaches that God hears the prayers of unbelievers; (4) This conflicts with centuries of Baptists' respect for every person's religious belief; (5) This is the stuff from which Holocausts come. I think the last point may have ignited the tinder. Paige Patterson came out just after that with his list of four liberals connected with Southern Baptist seminaries—I was one. I didn't really take that seriously. I mean, who was Paige Patterson?

DOOR: Yeah! Really!

GLENN: I met with Paige Patterson. At that time I heard he had been making noises about my book *Jesus Christ*, and so I asked him to meet with me and my D.Min. seminar and to discuss this. He did, and at that time he couldn't cite anything that he found wrong; but he later turned out to be taking quotations that I was refuting and presenting them as my views.

DOOR: So much for taking the Bible literally—what was that about "not bearing false witness"?

GLENN: These are very dishonest people; they are not the kind of people who are really interested in dealing with the truth. At any rate, from that time on I've been on the "hit" list.

DOOR: And they finally pushed you away from your Baptist tradition?

GLENN: The Baptist tradition has to do with the voluntary principle of religious liberty, separation of church and state, and voluntary association to carry out the mission of Christ. I thought all of these were endangered by what was happening in the Southern Baptist Convention, which had become the Catholic Church of the South— numerically so dominant that I could no longer consider myself Baptist in that way. As I saw it, I didn't really leave the Southern Baptist Convention; the Convention left the tradition that I belonged to.

DOOR: Then you're still a Baptist.

GLENN: I still see myself as very much a Baptist. Although I am a Bapto-Quakero-Methedo-Presbyterio-Lutherano-Episcopo-Catholic. The Baptist tradition depends on a minority consciousness. And having become the majority, Baptists in the South could no longer think like Baptists; they thought like medieval Catholics.

DOOR: Well, either that or like bigwig, power-hungry CEOs . . . .

GLENN: My first published article was in 1973, "How Far Can the Churches Go Using the Business Model as a Pattern for Church Life?" I pointed to a problem that I call "corporatism"—and this is a result of Baptists in the South growing up with American business. It goes back to just before the Civil War. The Transcontinental Railroad drove a spike in Odgen, Utah, in 1849, just on the heels of the forming of the Southern Baptist Convention, and Baptists in the South really got caught up in corporatist development. Gaines Dobbins at Southern Seminary became Professor of Church Efficiency and published a book, *The Efficient Church*, in 1923. He followed it up with subsequent books all based on this idea: Jesus was the "great entrepreneur." This whole thing—the church—is the most important business in the world; you have to operate it like a business. The Southern Baptist Convention would do anything to achieve the bottom line, which is always, of course, how many souls were saved; how many buildings are we building. Very pragmatic things.

DOOR: They never put it like this in our Baptist history lessons back in the days of Training Union on Sunday evenings.

GLENN: We need to take a new look at what the object of the Landmarkists was. The Landmarkists were really the farm crowd who had their reservations about the corporation model. And they were right! You keep on with this . . . it's a mentality that has serious moral problems. Mainly, you have to get rid of anybody who makes waves in the corporation. See, just like big business. Huge salaries, bonuses, everything. All that feeds into my ability to turn loose of the Southern Baptist connection.

DOOR: Did you have any connections with a young seminary student named Albert Mohler?

GLENN: *(laughs)* Interestingly, in 1982, Mohler asked me to serve as his Ph.D. Supervisor—he would have majored in church history. But I could not do it because I was going to Wake Forest. At any rate, up to that time when he would have been my student, there was no evidence that Mohler was a fundamentalist.

DOOR: So one of your former students is now the president of an institution where you aren't allowed to teach anymore. Yet you still live right next to Southern Seminary.

GLENN: Yes, it's a little uncomfortable. I don't know whether it's uncomfortable for me or for Mohler; it may be more uncomfortable for him. *(laughs)* But my backyard backs onto the campus.

DOOR: You've since been a part of two new seminaries—the Baptist Theological Seminary at Richmond and now the Baptist Seminary of Kentucky.

GLENN: Put them all together, there are at least a dozen of these moderate seminaries which have reacted to what happened with fundamentalist dominance of Southern Baptist seminaries. You always regret the changing of great institutions. Southern Baptist Theological Seminary has always been one of the most prestigious seminaries in the world.

DOOR: You sound a little mournful.

GLENN: I look on that with great regret. But it was a loss—such an important institution to these narrow-minded, parochial . . . . But on the other hand, there is something we have gained by having to form smaller seminaries where we can do things that are almost impossible to do in older, established seminaries. One is to emphasize spiritual formation for ministry as the heart as to what is being done. I think that must be seen as a plus.

DOOR: Back to Merton. How did he influence you?

GLENN: Living life informed by prayer out of this attentiveness to God in all of life. I put this together in my book *A Serious Call to a Contemplative Lifestyle.* That was in a way a tribute to the influence of Thomas Merton in my life.

DOOR: They say Merton had a great sense of humor.

GLENN: You know, had he not ended up at Gethsemani, he could have been Jay Leno.

DOOR: *The Tonight Show* with Thomas Merton—that'd be something worth watching! What do you think of the new Pope [Pope Benedict]?

GLENN: He seems to be confirming the worst fears that most had . . . essentially going back to the pre-Vatican II position, that the only true Christian faith is the Roman Catholic faith, and the only church you can rely on is the Roman Catholic Church, so he sounds sort of like the Southern Baptists, and I don't think that is very good.

DOOR: What do you think of President [George W.] Bush?

GLENN: Well, I'd like to have better thoughts about him than I do, but seeing "W" stickers on the backs of cars just sends me into a rage. I think he has put the country in grave danger. His awareness of the world situation is just abysmal. It's very hard for me to grasp that someone who has such a limited understanding of both the United States and the world could be elected president, but it happened. Will Campbell wrote me a note just after Bush was chosen by the Supreme Court: "Bush is too dumb to be so evil." *(laughs)* I haven't seen much that would correct his assessment. The way I assess it is—here is a guy who has failed in five businesses, and we have elected him to be head of the world's largest business, namely the United States government, and he has done to it what he has done to all five business *(laughs)*. And you look at the connection with "Kenny Boy" Lay of Enron. He has depended upon people of fuzzy ethical thinking.

DOOR: But at least he's open about his faith, huh?

GLENN: The sad thing is he's a Methodist. He has used this perverse understanding of Christianity which is focused on the agenda of the religious right . . . . I have always had a little ambivalence as to what extent religion should enter into politics. In our American model, we do not want the religious views of even the majority to determine decisions that are made affecting the civil welfare. Now I don't think separation is an absolute, but there is something like a wall of separation, using Jefferson's concept. There has to be. I think Bush has done his best to break down the separation of church and state. As people reflect on his presidency, I think it will be assessed as one of the worst, if not the worst, in American history. It's just almost incalculable the damage that has been done. Of course, I wouldn't favor impeaching Bush, because then we'd have Cheney! If we begin impeaching, begin with Cheney, then go up! *(laughs)*

DOOR: But now the Democrats are trying to "out-faith" the Republicans.

GLENN: I think that authentic faith does not stand on the street corner and pray; it does not make a big noise about its charities. I'm afraid that there is so much inauthentic where it is done for the wrong reasons. Authentic faith does what it does because of God, not to get elected into public office. I guess it's inevitable, but I would feel better if we had a good atheist. It is so demeaning of religion that this is happening. We have to blame it on the Republican use of the religious right.

DOOR: To be fair to Republicans, Jimmy Carter was the one who publicized that he was "born again."

GLENN: I think Jimmy Carter sort of started this trend of emphasizing his faith. But I think he's very genuine, as over against Bush . . . . You have to *live* your faith, not talk about it. What I see in Carter is someone who does live his faith, yet I wish he hadn't gotten this trend started. Then you had Reagan who used a lot of it . . . he was as I would characterize it a practical atheist, but he knew the buttons to push for the religious right. I think probably Mrs. Clinton is authentic. She'll represent a religious perspective that is close to a position represented by informed Methodism. I think there may be some genuineness about Obama—he's United Church of Christ in Chicago. I just wish that we could focus on the issues and not in terms of whether my god is stronger than your god.

DOOR: Are you hopeful for our nation and our world?

GLENN: Things look very bleak at the moment. But I'm hopeful, not because of what's being done by politicians. I think hope is in God. I think that if we look at the course of things and history, read the history of civilization, you have to feel very uncertain. What happened in the Roman Empire is happening in the United States now. When you talk about the decline and fall of the Roman Empire, you have to see some of those same things that are present which create concern. One, the Roman Empire had these great disparities with very few rich and the vast majority poor, where you had no middle class. Increasingly, we have no middle class. Things like that make me wonder about the future. We are over-consuming. The sort of thing Wendell Berry and others have pointed to.

DOOR: Excuse me, but can you pass the Prozac . . .

GLENN: I don't see great leadership. When you think at times we had great leaders come along to lead people through periods like this. But for America, we've had worse than the pits! Supposedly we are the one world power, and it's turned out to be nothing but a big fart!

DOOR: What is the one thing the world needs more of that it doesn't already have enough of?

GLENN: Saints! I think that basically, from the church's point of view, what we need to do is form saints—people of faith, hope, and love.

DOOR: And football! Wait, wrong Saints . . .

GLENN: I think fundamentalism is a movement that is frightened; instead of encouraging a search for God in the midst of life, it turns to absolutes . . . . If that sort of fear-ridden platform wins, then I think we have little hope of making it through. But if we can get people grounded on the reality of God in the midst of life, then I think we have hope. To quote Martin Luther King, Jr., "We don't know what the future holds, but we know who holds the future." That's the faith

I have to live by, with reference to my grandchildren. Looking at the world today, at the United States today . . . I feel anxious for them. But we have to trust God.

A Baptist Preacher Sits Down with Everyone's Favorite Deceased Monk

My Necro-Interview with Thomas Merton[1]

Inspired by an old *Wittenburg Door* "necro-interview" with the deceased Reinhold Niebuhr, I conducted my own such interview with the deceased monk, Thomas Merton. As I used direct quotes from Merton's books and journals, all of his words in the interview are exactly as they originally appeared, except for a few instances in which words were altered slightly to fit the format of the interview [as indicated in brackets]. There are also instances in which I added dialogue to help with transitions from questions to responses, as well as for some comic relief. These places are all noted with an asterisk (*). To minimize the amount of manipulation involved, I chose not to "gender-neutralize" Merton's responses, since including yet more parenthetical words would add to the already distracting brackets and asterisks.

Because I am aware that taking Merton's words out of their original context and interspersing them among my imaginary questions is risky business, I did my best to protect the meaning of his statements. However, what Merton has to say is as relevant today as ever—so I'll take that risk.[2]

One final note: it seems that even in death, Merton insists on being called "Tom."

BERT: I am interested in discovering how such a prophetic critic of the Church can remain a monk within the walls of one of the oldest institutions of all in Christianity—the Catholic Church. Let's begin with the Church and "the world." What did you leave behind when you left "the world" and entered the Abbey of Gethsemani?

TOM: As far as I can see, what I abandoned when I "left the world" and came to the monastery was the understanding of myself that I had developed in the context of civil society—my identification with what appeared to me to be its aims.

BERT: What about any money, status, possessions?

TOM: "The world" did not mean for me either riches—I was poor— or a life of luxury, certainly not the ambition to get somewhere in business or in anything else except writing. But it did mean a certain set of servitudes that I could no longer accept—servitudes to certain standards of value which to me were idiotic and repugnant and still are. . . . The image of a society that is happy because it drinks Coca-Cola or Seagrams or both and is protected by the bomb. The society that is imaged in the mass media and in advertising, in the movies, in TV, in best-sellers, in current fads, in all the pompous and trifling masks with which it hides callousness, sensuality, hypocrisy, cruelty, and fear.

BERT: As a Protestant, I'm accustomed to "the world" meaning things that we traditionally shun, like alcohol and sex. Your notion of "the world" is much broader, and much, much deeper. The Church often goes right along with and often participates fully with "the world" as you define it.

TOM: Yes. It is the same wherever you have mass man. . . . The materials and appearances differ, and in Western Europe perhaps the cut is a little more sophisticated. But it is the same suit of clothes, and same pair of ready-made pants, the same spiritual cretinism which in fact makes Christians and atheists indistinguishable.

BERT: If Christians are indistinguishable from nonbelievers in the world—because at the core we all share the same values, goals, and play by the same rules—doesn't that make loyalty to the Church, and even to faith itself, somewhat difficult?

TOM: My one real difficulty with faith is in really accepting the truth that the Church is a redeemed community . . . so that in fact to follow the mind of the Church is to be free from the mentality of the fallen society. Ideally I see this. But in fact there is so much that is not redeemed, and that seems to get into the thinking of those who represent the Church.

BERT: How does this make it difficult for you?

TOM: It is not easy to talk of prayer in a world where a President claims he prays for light in his decisions and then decides on genocidal attacks on a small nation. And where a Catholic Bishop praises this as a "work of love."

BERT: Yes, I know. We Baptists tend to rally around the way of the flag more than the way of the Cross. Faith tends to get shuffled behind our vision of "patriotism," since we celebrate our kind of faith as only being possible under these political circumstances.

TOM: Paralyzing incomprehension—what does one do when he realizes he is part of an organization whose members systematically try to "make a fool of God"? I suppose I begin by recognizing that I have done it as much as the best of them.

(laughter)

BERT: It is disturbing, though, how we Christians mix faith and politics so thoroughly, especially with regard to war.

TOM: What obsesses me most is the grim condition of the Church, committed in great part to the "escape clauses" that "justify" the brutalities of the secular solution, and which enable the moral theologian to hand over the ordinary Christian, bound hard and fast, to the power of the militarist. In the early days of Christianity, to be a soldier was abnormal, to refuse war was normal. Today, when war is beyond all reason, is utterly murderous and suicidal, we are told that the Christian who fails to participate is not a good Christian, he is evading his duty, rejecting the Cross!!! This is to me one of the most abominable and terrifying of signs. And one of the most convincingly awful indications that the end is near. In a word—that it may indeed be vitally necessary for us to be better Christians than our theologians, and that our very salvation may depend on this!

BERT: So, you're saying that the Church—in error—chooses the ways of the world in attempts to "fight" the ways of the world?

TOM: It was taken for granted that one contemned "the world" while seeking the same ends as the world, but with a different set of motives. Hence, what one contemned was in reality not "the world" as such, but a rival power structure or simply "our competitor." Contempt for the world became not contempt for the objectives of the world, but competition with the world on its own ground and for the same power, with contempt for its motives. Thus, in time, the "opposition" of "spiritual" and "secular" power has become in fact no more than the spirit of fraternal rivalry that exists—I presume—between Ford and General Motors.

BERT: This seems to make the Church into just another self-serving political party seeking more control and power than the other political parties.

TOM: Unconsciously the Church begins to concentrate too much on her own power and prestige rather than on her mission of service, preaching and love. She takes her institutional power too seriously as an essential means for fulfilling her function in the world, and as the world itself grows more and more arrogant and hostile to religion, the Church tends more and more to entrench herself in her power and to assert her claims against the world. Instead of serving the world, she struggles with it in order to preserve her influence in it. And in the struggle, her influence is in fact diminished, since people come less and less to expect from her anything but the truculent assertion of her right to their respect and their obedience, rather than the proclamation of the truth revealed to the world in Christ.

BERT: We're all just repeating Kierkegaard's *Attack Upon "Christendom,"* aren't we? It's like we've learned nothing over the past couple of centuries.

TOM: *Attack Upon "Christendom."* How can one laugh and shudder at the same time? The book is so incontrovertibly true. And to find myself a priest.

BERT: And me a pastor.

(laughter)

TOM: And to find [our] own [lives] so utterly false and trivial—in the light of the New Testament. And to look around [us] everywhere and find people desperately—or complacently—going through certain motions to prove that they are Christians.

BERT: Like slapping a "Jesus fish" on your car . . .

TOM: And far more people not giving a damn and not even paying attention, so that "proving one is a Christian" comes to mean begging for just a little attention from the world . . .

BERT: Notice my t-shirt; read my bumper sticker—hey, I'm a Christian!

TOM: But what can you do in the [twenty-first] century? We are becoming not only a Church of baroque seals and Renaissance chanceries, but of IBM machines!

BERT: And laptop computers and high-quality presentations in our state-of-the-art auditoriums.

TOM: People and energies are used up in triumphal projects that move nowhere, and only glorify the pompous ones who manage them. But this glory is no glory. No one pays any attention to it—except for those who, like [us], murmur and complain.

(laughter)

BERT: Are we being too harsh?

TOM: *(pausing)* This summary is of course grotesque and unfair. As a matter of fact, however, the problem is not as simple as all that. One finds a general agreement that the Church had better acquire a healthy and articulate respect for the modern world—otherwise she will have no place in it, except to be reduced to the level of fringe groups like Jehovah's Witnesses.

BERT: Christendom is gaining political power by using fear of "the world" as its primary platform, must like political parties use the fear of something—anything—to gain power. They act like the repression of the Middle Ages was a good thing—since the "church" was in charge.

TOM: Christendom is not the Church, of course. The Church is now in a world that is culturally "post-Christian." [Father] Tavard's idea is that, by turning to the world and working with those who are not explicitly Christian, we can perhaps in our convergence with them bring about a resurrection of basically Christian values in secular culture. Christianity can embrace the whole world without fear precisely because it is greater than the world.

BERT: So the Church does have a place and a role in the world, even after all of our complaints and criticisms?

TOM: Whether it is easy to love the Church, the Church as she is and not as she might be . . . . To love the "poor" sinners, yes. For we count ourselves among the poor ones. But the great, complacent, obtuse, powerful, and self-satisfied sinners who are aware only of their righteousness, who close the doors, who do not enter in and help others out, the Grand Inquisitors who build their own structure on top of God's structure and attach more importance to what they themselves have built than to what He builds . . . .

BERT: The rulers and managers of Christendom . . .

TOM: Yet they are in their own way patient and gentle. They too suffer. They too have a kind of humility. But they are closed. There are human realities to which they absolutely refuse to be sensitive. For they have somehow come to believe that a certain kind of compassion is a weakness they cannot afford.

BERT: And yet you manage to hang on inside the Church.

TOM: I have a friend named Rosemary who challenges my solitude.* There is a fundamental Christian honesty about her theology—its refusal to sweep evil under the rug and its "No" to phony incarnationalism. And above all she knows where the real problem lies: the Church. My feeling is that we shall not solve this problem ourselves (how could we? We are too much a part of it!), but events will bring on a crisis that will smash all façades. Maybe in the ruins of the great institutional idol we will recover something of our Christian truth.

BERT: You mentioned earlier the emerging "post-Christian" society in which we now live. Maybe this will bring the crisis that will smash the "institutional idol." In the meantime, what is our job, our purpose, our task at hand?

TOM: Our most important task is to become aware of the fact that our new consciousness of space no longer admits the traditional religious imagery by which we represent to ourselves our encounter with God. At the same time, we must also recognize that this traditional imagery was never essential to Christianity. We must recover the New Testament awareness that our God does not need a temple or even a cathedral. The New Testament teaches in fact that God has one indestructible temple: which is man himself. To understand that God is present in the world in man is in fact no new or radical idea. It is, on the contrary, one of the most elementary teachings of the New Testament.

BERT: There are more and more "postmodern/alternative" congregations emerging, which are free from traditional mainstream institutional structures and practices. There is a heavy emphasis on engaging the culture and, primarily, on experiencing the presence of God. They make great use of all the technology they can get their hands on: computers, projectors, movies, TV, rock music, etc. We want to make Church and God relevant—God Rocks!

TOM: A "God [Rocks!]" Church is no better, nor are the "God [Rocks!]" Christians an improvement over the others. Just the same established flippancy and triviality. And even more successful. They make a good living out of God's [relevance].

(laughter)

BERT: Some of them sure do! But there are many folks with, as you put it earlier, a healthy and articulate respect for contemporary culture, believing that the Church in fact does have a place in the culture. Are you against the increased use of technology and rock music?

TOM: I am averse to slogans, to the pressure people, to any unseemly eagerness to affirm that Christianity is great for boys [and girls] of the twenty-first Century. Why? Perhaps because I feel that they are trying, implicitly, to get others to serve their purposes, to inflate their egos for them?

BERT: Humility. Maybe that's what we all need.

TOM: What we need is a deeper understanding of Christ and of the mystery of His presence in the world, in man. From this we will gain a much truer, less arrogant, more humble and more merciful awareness of the true meaning of the Church and of her mission to man.

BERT: Contemplation may have a role in this emerging movement, much more so than in the previous manifestations of the Church as institutions of activities and power.

TOM: The Christian who is entirely concerned with external activities and temporal interests, not only does not desire contemplation, but he even makes himself incapable of knowing what it is. The only way to find out anything about the joys of contemplation is by experience. We must taste and see that the Lord is sweet.

BERT: This is what keeps you connected with the Church, isn't it? There's something about the Church that connects you with contemplation, and thus with the Eternal Christ.

TOM: *(lengthy pause)* By active participation in the liturgy the Christian prepares himself to enter into the Church's "contemplation" of the great mysteries of faith. . . . It involves man's whole being, body and soul, mind, will, imagination, emotion, and spirit. Worship takes man in his wholeness and consecrates him entirely to God, and thence contemplation is the perfection of worship. Without contemplation worship tends to remain lifeless and external.

BERT: We've gone from criticizing the Church for being too much like "the world" to the Church calling us out from "the world" and into the very Presence of God! Any more thoughts on this transforming role of the Church?

TOM: Sunday is a day of contemplation not because it is a day without work, a day when shops and banks and offices are closed, but because it is sacred to the mystery of the Resurrection. Sunday is the "Lord's Day" not in the sense that, on one day out of the week, one must stop and think of Him, but because it breaks into the ceaseless, "secular" round of time with a burst of light out of a sacred eternity. We stop working and rushing about on Sunday not only in order to rest up and start over again on Monday, but in order to collect our wits and realize the relative meaninglessness of the secular business which fills the other six days of the week, and taste the satisfaction of a peace which surpasses understanding and which is given us by Christ. Sunday reminds us of the peace that should filter through the whole week when our work is properly oriented.

BERT: Tom, you have a wonderful way with words—I wonder, could you conclude our interview with a meditative thought for other cynics like us to remember?

TOM: Let's see . . . How about this?* *(slight pause—Tom leans forward, eyebrows raised, and places his hand on my shoulder)* I believe in the Church. I am in the place where Christ has put me. Amen.

(long pause)

BERT: Amen. Thank you, again, Tom.

TOM: You're welcome.*

Notes

1. This was first published—with some editing differences—in the May/June 2006 issue of the *Wittenburg Door* magazine. It was my first published article for which I was paid. Originally written as an end-of-the-semester research paper for Dr. Glenn Hinson's seminary class on Merton, it was also published as an e-book short story by Faithlab. Thanks to Faithlab for granting permission for its use in this collection!

2. All of Merton's "answers" to my questions came from his books *Conjectures of a Guilty Bystander*, *The Inner Experience: Notes on Contemplation*, and his *Journals*, volumes IV, V, VI, VII. I encourage you to read these and other Merton books, and to enter into your own dialogue with Fr. Louis.

Afterword

Musings on the Guy Whom Some People Know as "Bert"

Although he is not as widely recognized as he should be, Daniel Bailey is an extremely gifted young musician and songwriter who lives in Nashville. The raw honesty of his lyrics and his strong stage presence combine to make his performances memorable and enjoyable, and his songs can stick with you for years, once you listen to them. It was at a concert where Daniel opened for The Lost Dogs that he met a young Bert Montgomery, and was later able to rise to infamy by performing both roving concerts with Bert and semi-stable ones at a church somewhere in Mississippi that is filled with people who have the temerity to claim Bert as their pastor.

There is no truth to the rumor that Bert named his son Daniel after Mr. Bailey, which is why I never started such a rumor, but if there was, it would make for a great story. There may, however, be some truth to the rumor that Bert has a habit of hanging around great and famous people in hopes that some of their greatness and fame may rub off on him. He has gone to such great lengths to pursue this that he even once traveled back in time to "interview" Thomas Merton, and he has been known in the past to associate himself with Johnny Cash while claiming to channel, in some way, people like Willie Nelson, Elvis, and Glenn Hinson. There are, of course, other celebrities that Bert has approached in some way, and you undoubtedly read more about that in this book.

I first became aware of Bert when he came to me seeking to be America's Next Great Youth Minister. This was, of course, pure fantasy, since any great youth minister would toil away in obscurity and later wonder where his or her life went wrong. Bert soon repented of this error and later found himself working in another job for which he feels inadequate: being a pastor. Of course, those feelings of inadequacy are what make him so good at what he does, and it is serving that vocation that has led him, Jency, Rob, and Daniel on a wild and often perilous life journey.

Setting aside, for the moment, that he is a surprise, surprised, and surprising pastor, Bert has long had a desire to minister to people who do things in music and help them find themselves as musicians and ministers to the human soul. This may go back to Bert's days as a heavy-metal musician—and I have seen pictures where he has been carrying a heavy-metal musical instrument. Aren't trombones heavy? At least compared to some other instruments people carry? As I think he explained it to me one day, being someone who goes on stage can isolate you and make it difficult for you to find authenticity, whether in others or in yourself. People who are in such situations practically cry out for ministry, yet no one seems to see them in that way quite like Bert does. Seeing a need for care that no one is meeting is, actually, a hallmark of good ministry. The best of us look for heartbreaking things and/or broken people, feel our own hearts break, and look for ways to address the issue. Many of us would question whether such a ministry is even possible, but I think that you will see from his writing that Bert has gradually found his way, just as he has also found his way as a pastor to small local churches. Much of what he does "kind of happens," and that's a beautiful thing.

When I'm not berating Bert (did I call him a "stinky hippy" anywhere in this piece yet? Well, I have now . . .), making jokes at his expense, or otherwise expressing outright amazement that he may actually amount to something, I am privileged to be able to discuss with him various issues that arise in practicing the craft of writing. In plainer language, thanks to Bert, I read a lot of wonderfully weird stuff and frequently have to put on my "editor" hat. Sometimes I even get to go on the Internet and fight off critics for him, which is about as much fun as you can have in a discussion group. I actually do this for a lot of young writers, but Bert is special in that he sets an example for seminary students and others who may someday want to do this kind of writing. Many beginning writers, especially at the academic level, struggle with the idea that they have something to say. They get so caught up in what they think people want to hear, or how they want to hear it, that they forget to be who they are. As Bert fled one seminary for a better one, he brought this attitude with him as well, and he seemed to handcuff his writing in order to stuff it into a mold that he thought it had to fit. At some point, he was able both to hear people telling him that he didn't have to do that and to believe it strongly enough to make a leap of faith and start writing like Bert, instead of just being a student. I'd like to say that this transformed his seminary experience, and maybe it did, but in my case it didn't improve his classroom performance so much as make his papers exceedingly interesting to read.

That's a lesson that a number of writers need to learn. The kinds of people who are concerned with your "correctness" have other problems that they need to get over, too. Don't write for them. Say what you really feel, and say it in creative and interesting ways. Work at the craft of saying things your way instead of trying to fit someone else's idea of propriety. Tell the stories that people need to hear instead of just the stories they want to hear. Most important, understand that everything that happens in your life can teach you and your readers something, if you're willing to let it. Stories drawn from your experiences are critically important because of this, and the people who read them and retell them can be enriched by them if they will let themselves be enriched.

Bert is one of those rare writers who seems to understand all of this deep in his bones. Because of this, some people—perhaps you, too— choose to be offended by the things he writes, which often ask questions we're not supposed to ask and strike a lot closer to home than we want them to. The more I read his material, the more I think of Bert as someone who asks, in essence, "What if we really believed all the things we say we believe and really lived according to the standards we say we have?"—much like a child who didn't know that such questions shouldn't be asked in "polite company." While you might enjoy, or hate, reading the things he has to say, or possibly just disregard them as "unworkable" or "naive," you need to read them and think about them. As anyone who has visited a good counselor knows, there can be great therapeutic value in having someone challenge your assumptions and force you to reconsider your comfortable worldview. Whatever else you might think about Bert, you at least have to admit that he is challenging!

—*David Adams*
Professor of Christian Education
Baptist Seminary of Kentucky
December 2013

Other available titles from SMYTH& HELWYS®

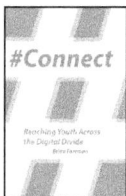

#Connect
Reaching Youth Across the Digital Divide
Brian Foreman

Reaching our youth across the digital divide is a struggle for parents, ministers, and other adults who work with Generation Z— today's teenagers. *#Connect* leads readers into the technological landscape, encourages conversations with teenagers, and reminds us all to be the presence of Christ in every facet of our lives.   *978-1-57312-693-9 120 pages/pb* **$13.00**

1 Corinthians (Smyth & Helwys Annual Bible Study series)
Growing through Diversity
Don & Anita Flowers

Don and Anita Flowers present this comprehensive study of 1 Corinthians, filled with scholarly insight and dealing with such varied topics as marriage and sexuality, spiritual gifts and love, and diversity and unity. The authors examine Paul's relationship with the church in Corinth as well as the culture of that city to give context to topics that can seem far removed from Christian life today.   *Teaching Guide 978-1-57312-701-1 122 pages/pb* **$14.00**

Study Guide 978-1-57312-705-9 52 pages/pb **$6.00**

Beyond the American Dream
Millard Fuller

In 1968, Millard finished the story of his journey from pauper to millionaire to home builder. His wife, Linda, occasionally would ask him about getting it published, but Millard would reply, "Not now. I'm too busy." This is that story.   *978-1-57312-563-5 272 pages/pb* **$20.00**

Blissful Affliction
The Ministry and Misery of Writing
Judson Edwards

Edwards draws from more than forty years of writing experience to explore why we use the written word to change lives and how to improve the writing craft.   *978-1-57312-594-9 144 pages/pb* **$15.00**

To order call **1-800-747-3016** or visit **www.helwys.com**

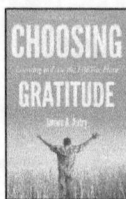

Choosing Gratitude
Learning to Love the Life You Have
James A. Autry

Autry reminds us that gratitude is a choice, a spiritual—not social—process. He suggests that if we cultivate gratitude as a way of being, we may not change the world and its ills, but we can change our response to the world. If we fill our lives with moments of gratitude, we will indeed love the life we have.   *978-1-57312-614-4 144 pages/pb* **$15.00**

Choosing Gratitude 365 Days a Year
Your Daily Guide to Grateful Living
James A. Autry and Sally J. Pederson

Filled with quotes, poems, and the inspired voices of both Pederson and Autry, in a society consumed by fears of not having "enough"—money, possessions, security, and so on—this book suggests that if we cultivate gratitude as a way of being, we may not change the world and its ills, but we can change our response to the world.   *978-1-57312-689-2 210 pages/pb* **$18.00**

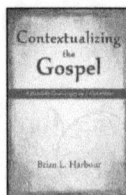

Contextualizing the Gospel
A Homiletic Commentary on 1 Corinthians
Brian L. Harbour

Harbour examines every part of Paul's letter, providing a rich resource for those who want to struggle with the difficult texts as well as the simple texts, who want to know how God's word—all of it—intersects with their lives today.   *978-1-57312-589-5 240 pages/pb* **$19.00**

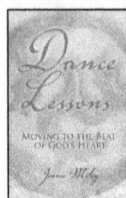

Dance Lessons
Moving to the Beat of God's Heart
Jeanie Miley

Miley shares her joys and struggles a she learns to "dance" with the Spirit of the Living God.   *978-1-57312-622-9 240 pages/pb* **$19.00**

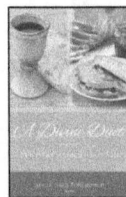

A Divine Duet
Ministry and Motherhood
Alicia Davis Porterfield, ed.

Each essay in this inspiring collection is as different as the mother-minister who wrote it, from theologians to chaplains, inner-city ministers to rural-poverty ministers, youth pastors to preachers, mothers who have adopted, birthed, and done both.

          978-1-57312-676-2 146 pages/pb **$16.00**

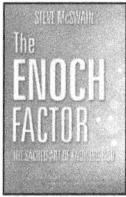

The Enoch Factor
The Sacred Art of Knowing God
Steve McSwain

The Enoch Factor is a persuasive argument for a more enlightened religious dialogue in America, one that affirms the goals of all religions—guiding followers in self-awareness, finding serenity and happiness, and discovering what the author describes as "the sacred art of knowing God." 978-1-57312-556-7 *256 pages/pb* **$21.00**

Ethics as if Jesus Mattered
Essays in Honor of Glen H. Stassen
Rick Axtell, Michelle Tooley, Michael L. Westmoreland-White, eds.

Ethics as if Jesus Mattered will introduce Stassen's work to a new generation, advance dialogue and debate in Christian ethics, and inspire more faithful discipleship just as it honors one whom the contributors consider a mentor. 978-1-57312-695-3 *234 pages/pb* **$18.00**

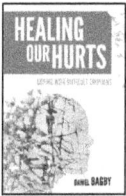

Healing Our Hurts
Coping with Difficult Emotions
Daniel Bagby

In *Healing Our Hurts*, Daniel Bagby identifies and explains all the dynamics at play in these complex emotions. Offering practical biblical insights to these feelings, he interprets faith-based responses to separate overly religious piety from true, natural human emotion. This book helps us learn how to deal with life's difficult emotions in a redemptive and responsible way. 978-1-57312-613-7 *144 pages/pb* **$15.00**

Help! I Teach Youth Sunday School
Brian Foreman, Bo Prosser, and David Woody

Real-life stories are mingled with information on Youth and their culture, common myths about Sunday School, a new way of preparing the Sunday school lesson, creative teaching ideas, ways to think about growing a class, and how to reach out for new members and reach in to old members. 1-57312-427-3 *128 pages/pb* **$14.0**

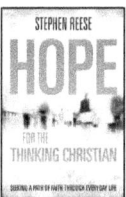

Hope for the Thinking Christian
Seeking a Path of Faith through Everyday Life
Stephen Reese

Readers who want to confront their faith more directly, to think it through and be open to God in an individual, authentic, spiritual encounter will find a resonant voice in Stephen Reese.
978-1-57312-553-6 *160 pages/pb* **$16.00**

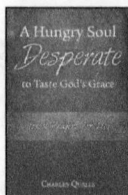

A Hungry Soul Desperate to Taste God's Grace
Honest Prayers for Life
Charles Qualls

Part of how we *see* God is determined by how we *listen* to God. There is so much noise and movement in the world that competes with images of God. This noise would drown out God's beckoning voice and distract us. Charles Qualls's newest book offers readers prayers for that journey toward the meaning and mystery of God. *978-1-57312-648-9 152 pages/pb* **$14.00**

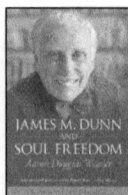

James M. Dunn and Soul Freedom
Aaron Douglas Weaver

James Milton Dunn, over the last fifty years, has been the most aggressive Baptist proponent for religious liberty in the United States. Soul freedom—voluntary, uncoerced faith and an unfettered individual conscience before God—is the basis of his understanding of church-state separation and the historic Baptist basis of religious liberty. *978-1-57312-590-1 224 pages/pb* **$18.00**

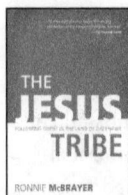

The Jesus Tribe
Following Christ in the Land of the Empire
Ronnie McBrayer

The Jesus Tribe fleshes out the implications, possibilities, contradictions, and complexities of what it means to live within the Jesus Tribe and in the shadow of the American Empire.

978-1-57312-592-5 208 pages/pb **$17.00**

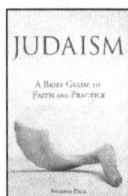

Judaism
A Brief Guide to Faith and Practice
Sharon Pace

Sharon Pace's newest book is a sensitive and comprehensive introduction to Judaism. What is it like to be born into the Jewish community? How does belief in the One God and a universal morality shape the way in which Jews see the world? How does one find meaning in life and the courage to endure suffering? How does one mark joy and forge community ties? *978-1-57312-644-1 144 pages/pb* **$16.00**

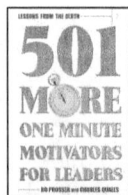

Lessons from the Cloth 2
501 More One Minute Motivators for Leaders
Bo Prosser and Charles Qualls

As the force that drives organizations to accomplishment, leadership is at a crucial point in churches, corporations, families, and almost every arena of life. In this follow-up to their first volume, Prosser and Qualls will inspire you to keep growing in your leadership career.

978-1-57312-665-6 152 pages/pb **$11.00**

To order call **1-800-747-3016** or visit **www.helwys.com**

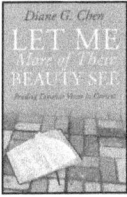

Let Me More of Their Beauty See
Reading Familiar Verses in Context
Diane G. Chen

Let Me More of Their Beauty See offers eight examples of how attention to the historical and literary settings can safeguard against taking a text out of context, bring out its transforming power in greater dimension, and help us apply Scripture appropriately in our daily lives.

978-1-57312-564-2 *160 pages/pb* **$17.00**

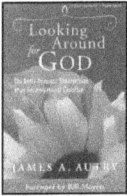

Looking Around for God
The Strangely Reverent Observations of an Unconventional Christian
James A. Autry

Looking Around for God, Autry's tenth book, is in many ways his most personal. In it he considers his unique life of faith and belief in God. Autry is a former Fortune 500 executive, author, poet, and consultant whose work has had a significant influence on leadership thinking.

978-157312-484-3 *144 pages/pb* **$16.00**

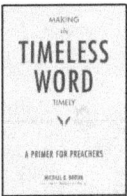

Making the Timeless Word Timely
A Primer for Preachers
Michael B. Brown

Michael Brown writes, "There is a simple formula for sermon preparation that creates messages that apply and engage whether your parish is rural or urban, young or old, rich or poor, five thousand members or fifty." The other part of the task, of course, involves being creative and insightful enough to know how to take the general formula for sermon preparation and make it particular in its impact on a specific congregation. Brown guides the reader through the formula and the skills to employ it with excellence and integrity.

978-1-57312-578-9 *160 pages/pb* **$16.00**

Meeting Jesus Today
For the Cautious, the Curious, and the Committed
Jeanie Miley

Meeting Jesus Today, ideal for both individual study and small groups, is intended to be used as a workbook. It is designed to move readers from studying the Scriptures and ideas within the chapters to recording their journey with the Living Christ.

978-1-57312-677-9 *320 pages/pb* **$19.00**

To order call **1-800-747-3016** or visit **www.helwys.com**

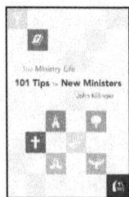

The Ministry Life
101 Tips for New Ministers
John Killinger

Sharing years of wisdom from more than fifty years in ministry and teaching, *The Ministry Life: 101 Tips for New Ministers* by John Killinger is filled with practical advice and wisdom for a minister's day-to-day tasks as well as advice on intellectual and spiritual habits to keep ministers of any age healthy and fulfilled.   *978-1-57312-662-5 244 pages/pb* **$19.00**

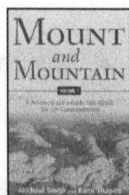

Mount and Mountain
Vol. 1: A Reverend and a Rabbi Talk About the Ten Commandments
Rami Shapiro and Michael Smith

Mount and Mountain represents the first half of an interfaith dialogue—a dialogue that neither preaches nor placates but challenges its participants to work both singly and together in the task of reinterpreting sacred texts. Mike and Rami discuss the nature of divinity, the power of faith, the beauty of myth and story, the necessity of doubt, the achievements, failings, and future of religion, and, above all, the struggle to live ethically and in harmony with the way of God.   *978-1-57312-612-0 144 pages/pb* **$15.00**

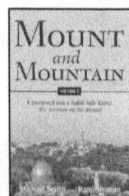

Mount and Mountain
Vol. 2: A Reverend and a Rabbi Talk About the Sermon on the Mount
Rami Shapiro and Michael Smith

This book, focused on the Sermon on the Mount, represents the second half of Mike and Rami's dialogue. In it, Mike and Rami explore the text of Jesus' sermon cooperatively, contributing perspectives drawn from their lives and religious traditions and seeking moments of illumination.   *978-1-57312-654-0 254 pages/pb* **$19.00**

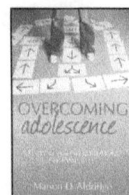

Overcoming Adolescence
Growing Beyond Childhood into Maturity
Marion D. Aldridge

In *Overcoming Adolescence*, Marion D. Aldridge poses questions for adults of all ages to consider. His challenge to readers is one he has personally worked to confront: to grow up *all the way*—mentally, physically, academically, socially, emotionally, and spiritually. The key involves not only knowing how to work through the process but also how to recognize what may be contributing to our perpetual adolescence.

978-1-57312-577-2 156 pages/pb **$17.00**

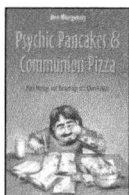

Psychic Pancakes & Communion Pizza
More Musings and Mutterings of a Church Misfit
Bert Montgomery

Psychic Pancakes & Communion Pizza is Bert Montgomery's highly anticipated follow-up to *Elvis, Willie, Jesus & Me* and contains further reflections on music, film, culture, life, and finding Jesus in the midst of it all.   *978-1-57312-578-9 160 pages/pb* **$16.00**

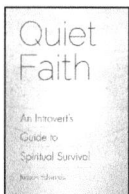

Quiet Faith
An Introvert's Guide to Spiritual Survival
Judson Edwards

In eight finely crafted chapters, Edwards looks at key issues like evangelism, interpreting the Bible, dealing with doubt, and surviving the church from the perspective of a confirmed, but sometimes reluctant, introvert. In the process, he offers some provocative insights that introverts will find helpful and reassuring.   *978-1-57312-681-6 144 pages/pb* **$15.00**

Reading Ezekiel (Reading the Old Testament series)
A Literary and Theological Commentary
Marvin A. Sweeney

The book of Ezekiel points to the return of YHWH to the holy temple at the center of a reconstituted Israel and creation at large. As such, the book of Ezekiel portrays the purging of Jerusalem, the Temple, and the people, to reconstitute them as part of a new creation at the conclusion of the book. With Jerusalem, the Temple, and the people so purged, YHWH stands once again in the holy center of the created world.

978-1-57312-658-8 264 pages/pb **$22.00**

Reading Hosea–Micah
(Reading the Old Testament series)
A Literary and Theological Commentary
Terence E. Fretheim

Terence E. Fretheim explores themes of indictment, judgment, and salvation in Hosea–Micah. The indictment against the people of God especially involves issues of idolatry, as well as abuse of the poor and needy. The effects of such behaviors are often horrendous in their severity. While God is often the subject of such judgments, the consequences, like fruit, grow out of the deed itself.   *978-1-57312-687-8 224 pages/pb* **$22.00**

To order call **1-800-747-3016** or visit **www.helwys.com**

Reading Samuel (Reading the Old Testament series)
A Literary and Theological Commentary
Johanna W. H. van Wijk-Bos

Interpreted masterfully by preeminent Old Testament scholar Johanna W. H. van Wijk-Bos, the story of Samuel touches on a vast array of subjects that make up the rich fabric of human life. The reader gains an inside look at leadership, royal intrigue, military campaigns, occult practices, and the significance of religious objects of veneration.

978-1-57312-607-6 272 pages/pb **$22.00**

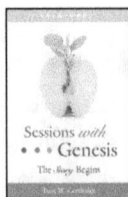

Sessions with Genesis (Session Bible Studies series)
The Story Begins
Tony W. Cartledge

Immersing us in the book of Genesis, Tony W. Cartledge examines both its major stories and the smaller cycles of hope and failure, of promise and judgment. Genesis introduces these themes of divine faithfulness and human failure in unmistakable terms, tracing Israel's beginning to the creation of the world and professing a belief that Israel's particular history had universal significance.

978-1-57312-636-6 144 pages/pb **$14.00**

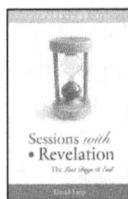

Sessions with Revelation (Session Bible Studies series)
The Final Days of Evil
David Sapp

David Sapp's careful guide through Revelation demonstrates that it is a letter of hope for believers; it is less about the last days of history than it is about the last days of evil. Without eliminating its mystery, Sapp unlocks Revelation's central truths so that its relevance becomes clear.

978-1-57312-706-6 166 pages/pb **$14.00**

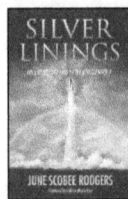

Silver Linings
My Life Before and After *Challenger 7*
June Scobee Rodgers

We know the public story of *Challenger 7*'s tragic destruction. That day, June's life took a new direction that ultimately led to the creation of the Challenger Center and to new life and new love. Her story of Christian faith and triumph over adversity will inspire readers of every age.

978-1-57312-570-3 352 pages/hc **$28.00**

978-1-57312-694-6 352 pages/pb **$18.00**

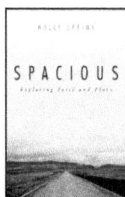

Spacious
Exploring Faith and Place
Holly Sprink

Exploring where we are and why that matters to God is an ongoing process. If we are present and attentive, God creatively and continuously widens our view of the world.   978-1-57312-649-6 156 pages/pb **$16.00**

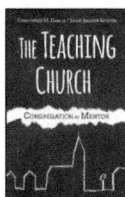

The Teaching Church
Congregation as Mentor
Christopher M. Hamlin / Sarah Jackson Shelton

Collected in *The Teaching Church: Congregation as Mentor* are the stories of the pastors who shared how congregations have shaped, nurtured, and, sometimes, broken their resolve to be faithful servants of God.   978-1-57312-682-3 112 pages/pb **$13.00**

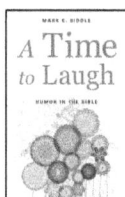

A Time to Laugh
Humor in the Bible
Mark E. Biddle

An extension of his well-loved seminary course on humor in the Bible, *A Time to Laugh* draws on Mark E. Biddle's command of Hebrew language and cultural subtleties to explore the ways humor was intentionally incorporated into Scripture. With characteristic liveliness, Biddle guides the reader through the stories of six biblical characters who did rather unexpected things.   978-1-57312-683-0 164 pages/pb **$14.00**

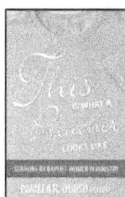

This Is What a Preacher Looks Like
Sermons by Baptist Women in Ministry
Pamela Durso, ed.

In this collection of sermons by thirty-six Baptist women, their voices are soft and loud, prophetic and pastoral, humorous and sincere. They are African American, Asian, Latina, and Caucasian. They are sisters, wives, mothers, grandmothers, aunts, and friends.

978-1-57312-554-3 144 pages/pb **$18.00**

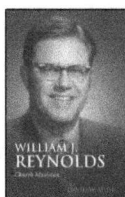

William J. Reynolds
Church Musician
David W. Music

William J. Reynolds is renowned among Baptist musicians, music ministers, song leaders, and hymnody students. In eminently readable style, David W. Music's comprehensive biography describes Reynolds's family and educational background, his career as a minister of music, denominational leader, and seminary professor.   978-1-57312-690-8 358 pages/pb **$23.00**

To order call **1-800-747-3016** or visit **www.helwys.com**